Mel Heimer

THE
LONG
COUNT

Atheneum   *New York*

1969

I lift my glass in a grateful toast
To those glorious days of the used-to-be—
Days that live on in memory,
Bathed in a shimmering golden haze—

                    John Irving Dillon

ILLUSTRATIONS

Follow page 118

Jack Dempsey
(Brown Brothers)

Tex Rickard, boxing's greatest promoter
(Brown Brothers)

The crowd at the Dempsey-Carpentier fight, 1921
(Brown Brothers)

The Dempsey-Carpentier fight, 1921
(United Press International Photo)

The Dempsey-Gibbons fight, 1923
(Brown Brothers)

The Tunney-Gibbons fight, 1925
(Brown Brothers)

Tunney goes down for the long count, 1927
(Brown Brothers)

Dempsey and Tunney during the long count, 1927
(Wide World Photos)

Dempsey down in the 8th in the long-count fight, 1927
(United Press International Photo)

Jack Dempsey supervises Rudolph Valentino's boxing lesson
(United Press International Photo)

Gene Tunney and George Bernard Shaw
(United Press International Photo)

Gene Tunney
(Bettmann Archive)

THE LONG COUNT

CHAPTER 1

THIS WAS THURSDAY, September 23, 1926, in Philadelphia. There have been wetter and more uncomfortable nights, but this one would do, as the poker players say, for openers.

It had been raining for the better part of a half-hour on the outskirts of the city, and in the big sports stadium called the Sesquicentennial, slightly more that 120,000 people were pushing, shoving and inching their way along, trying to get out and go home. There was no cover to the stadium. The rain beat down, and men's broad-brimmed fedora hats slowly softened into shapeless bits of sogginess. The women's short skirts were plastered against their legs until you could see the bumpy little hoops where their stockings had been rolled.

The downpour seemed unending, and its squishy, steady sound softened the noise, the yelling, the clack of shoes on concrete. Around the twenty-foot prize ring, now past the stage of mere wetness, now speckled here and there with pools of rain water, the paunchy sportswriters tried to shovel damp sheets of paper into their typewriters, tried to type, said ah the hell with it, and turned to their telegraphers and slowly, miserably, dictated their stories. Gentle, portly Grantland Rice, their dean, simply was trying to elbow his way out of the stadium and get to shelter. He had a couple of hours' grace for his story, which was for the next day's afternoon papers, and he was going to fashion it back at his midtown hotel. He planned to, that is. When he got there, he would find that a sore throat had worsened and a hangover had not improved, and a saturnine, now-sour man named Ring Lardner would do his chore for him.

All of the others were there—Paul Gallico, Westbrook Pegler, Jim Dawson, W. O. McGeehan, even Elmer Davis . . . and a petite, pretty redhead named Katharine Brush, who looked at Pegler in the darkness of the wet night and maybe, just maybe, felt in her head the stirring of the story that was to become *Young Man of Manhattan,* which was to begin with this very night. Maybe Miss Brush was to tell it best: "It was the sort of fight night nobody enjoys save those who were unable to be present. They tell you afterward, smugly, 'Well, we thought of you! There we were, all warm and cosy, hearing it *perfectly* on the radio. . . .' "

To BEGIN WITH, to *really* begin with, you must understand that this was a different, one-of-a-kind world.

4

There were 120,757 spectators in Sesquicentennial Stadium that night. They paid $1,895,723 for admission —and not one among them, nor among the millions who sat in living rooms and speak-easies listening to the radio, thought there was anything bizarre or outlandish about such figures. Of *course* 120,000 people would pay to see Jack Dempsey and Gene Tunney. Wouldn't you? For the world's *heavyweight* championship?

It was a world in which such things were of almost vital importance. This was the generation of the Twenties, fabled in story and song, as they say, and earmarked by some as the personal property of Hemingway and Fitzgerald. There were no world affairs worth speaking of. Oh, perhaps they were there and they were happening, all right, but only a handful of double-domes knew of them. People, instead, talked of whether Arthur Brisbane was right when he said a gorilla could defeat a man, whether Shipwreck Kelly could break his flagpole-sitting record and whether Frances "Peaches" Heenan's marriage to Daddy Browning really was consummated. Communism, civil rights, ideologies, man's injustice to man—there were none of these. The world had just ended the war to end all wars and now it was on a monstrous bender.

The earth spun a little more dizzily than usual. Its historians were newsmen with press cards in their hatbands, brims pushed backward, beautiful professional snoopers who, for at least once in their lives, were allowed full rein for their wry cynicism—men who knew that every train you take goes off the rails, every ship sinks, and that as long as you have to make the trip, you might as well take Wilson Mizner's advice and remem-

5

ber to smell the daisies. The password in the Twenties, for sure, was: you only go this way once, so vo-do-de-o-do.

On this September 23? Well, in the Deep South, Floridians and others in the Gulf states were digging out of the wreckage of a tremendous hurricane that killed more than five hundred persons, and the meteorology people were saying the storm might curve north and bring bad weather to the big fight, which already had pushed the hurricane from page one. In the Rhineland, long years after the end of the "Great War," the French finally were beginning to evacuate their seven thousand occupation troops, and the big news out of Washington was that, from now on, only total abstainers would be allowed to work in the Federal Prohibition Service.

At Franklin Simon & Co., one of Manhattan's better stores, you could buy a choice pair of men's shoes for $8 and the women's ads dealt in cloches, dresses with no waistlines and "exclusive copies" of Patou and Molyneux originals. Mrs. Matthew Astor Wilks, who had lived for years in Hoboken, New Jersey, in a $19-a-month tenement flat with her mother, Hetty Green, the world's richest woman, signed to rent a whole floor of a new apartment building at 988 Fifth Avenue at $11,000 a year. The Broadway Limited was announcing proudly to the world that it made the New York–Chicago run in twenty hours. In West Orange, New Jersey, Thomas Alva Edison pontificated for publication that, so far as music was concerned, "radio is a failure; the sound is too distorted."

THE SEPTEMBER NIGHT in Philadelphia, then, was one of the passing daisies to be smelled—and, too, it was the

coming together at long last of two professional fist fighters whose lives over a half-dozen years and more had
been verging closer and closer, like parallel lines merging
on the horizon.

One, the man Dempsey, was from the Far West, from
the town of Manassa in southern Colorado, which lay in
the San Luis Valley, a flat, high-lying plain 100 miles
long and 70 miles across, surrounded by mountains
reaching up to 14,000 feet. He was the ninth child of
parents who had come west from the West Virginia
mountains.

Gene Fowler, who had known him in the early days
around Denver, remembered that "He never liked to fight
then. He was the nicest kid in the neighborhood." Dempsey had grown up the hard way, riding the rods and then
turning to fighting to make a dollar—"You could hit me
on the chin with a sledge hammer. When you haven't
eaten for two days, you'll understand"—and at last had
become the most famous of boxers, married to a movie
star, making fabulous purses and becoming, in the words
of his arch-foe Tunney, a person "who had the most bind-
ing cords of association with the public of any man." In
the ring, the sportswriter Rice said, he was "the oddest
mixture of humanity I've known. He was a killer—a
superhuman wild man. His teeth were frequently bared
and his complete intent was an opponent's destruction.
He was a fighter—one who used every trick to wreck the
other fighter."

A little rococo, a little purple around the edges, a little
melodramatic, this prose . . . yet this was the Twenties.
Prizefighters were written of in this fashion.

The other, the man Tunney, was born across the country from Dempsey, in a downtown Manhattan flat over a

grocery store, and raised in Greenwich Village—a city kid whose naïveté and almost righteous air seemed to jar with the early juvenile sophistication of the other street Arabs. At fifteen he got a job as an office boy in a steamship company for five dollars a week, and a few years later as a United States Marine he won the light-heavyweight championship of the Army Expeditionary Force in Europe, before Belgium's King Albert, General John J. Pershing and France's Marshal Foch.

Where Dempsey was outgoing, warm, humorous and given to downrating himself candidly, Tunney was much more serious. He borrowed and read *A Winter's Tale* while a Marine in Europe, "until I finally got the meter, not as intelligently as I wanted but enough to know what was going on." The tendency of the day was to scoff at him as a Shakespearean student, to dismiss it as publicity, to hoot at his meeting and correspondence with George Bernard Shaw. But at thirteen, in St. Veronica's School in the Village, he had acted in undergraduate plays and could recite the speeches of Portia, Antonio and Shylock with relative ease.

This man, then, who provided the other half of the drama on that wet autumn night in Philadelphia, grew up, too, to be a fist fighter—but of a different kind. He made himself into a cool, calculating boxer who enjoyed the rudimentary strategy of the sport but little else about it, who had turned to fighting only because it was a way out of the meager, threadbare existence of downtown New York. The one, the Westerner—the natural. The other, the city kid—the boy who found himself in an unnatural medium and made the best of it.

* * *

FOR TUNNEY the big fight was the climax, the raising of Land's End. Six years before, he had met Dempsey on a ferry crossing the Hudson River, and during the twenty-minute ride the champion had kidded and talked with him and been totally gracious—and during it all, the ex-Marine had been thinking, unable to stop himself, that one day he would fight this man and beat him.

A year or two after that chance meeting, Tunney had fought a preliminary bout on the program in Boyle's Thirty Acres in Jersey City, where the feature was the "Battle of the Century," in which Dempsey, still reasonably the tigerlike "killer of the ring" who had whipped Willard so impressively for the title in 1919, knocked out Georges Carpentier, an overgrown middleweight from France. That night Tunney's fight was against a fighter named Soldier Jones, and Gene knocked him out in seven rounds. A sportswriter spoke to Gene after the bout. "What are your plans?" he asked.

"My plans are all Dempsey," Tunney said flatly.

"Well, what about Harry Greb, Carpentier, Tommy Gibbons and so on?"

"I suppose I'll have to beat them on my way up," the other said, "but Dempsey is the one I want."

A year or two before 1926, Tunney had played golf in Florida with Tommy Armour, the Scottish professional, and the fighter had hit his drives and then run down the fairway, shadowboxing, hooking, jabbing, throwing phantom punch combinations, and muttering, "Dempsey, Dempsey!" Perhaps it was not an obsession, but it was awfully close.

To Dempsey, Tunney was just another boxer, someone to nod to pleasantly in the street and then try to ruin in the ring because that was his business. Only the champion, of all the people involved, knew he wasn't the same man in 1926 who had beaten Willard in 1919. Almost, but almost wasn't good enough. The living had been easy, the days and months and years had been soft; Dempsey still felt he could overpower Tunney, but, as he later said, "for a few years I remained nearly as formidable as I had been in 1918 and 1919. Then I began to slip faster and faster. Curiously enough, as my ability declined, my reputation grew." And so it did. The world of America accepted it; Dempsey was the invincible.

Even Tunney almost accepted it . . . until one night, weeks before the championship bout, he had a nightmare about Dempsey thrashing him and he awoke, sweating and shaky, and told himself that this never would do. That night in training camp may have been, really, when Dempsey lost his title. Tunney told himself there were no two ways about it, he had to be not afraid of the other. And because he had channeled his own life so decisively and firmly, that was the way it was. As he told the sportswriters just before the fight, "What can happen to me? All I can get is a sock on the jaw—and I'm not afraid of that."

THERE WAS no doubt that, coming up to the Philadelphia meeting, Tunney had honed himself into sharp mental and physical condition and Dempsey was rusty.

Part of the blame for Dempsey's shape belonged to Tex Rickard, the onetime Yukon gold-rush hustler and promoter who controlled big-league boxing. After Dempsey defeated Luis Angel Firpo in a sensational fight in 1924, Rickard—knowing the value of suspense and build-up—cautioned the champion, "Don't fight too often." For a long time, then, Dempsey engaged only in exhibition matches. His razor edge vanished. Maybe Rickard didn't care. Maybe he thought it was time for a new champion, although Dempsey had been a personal gold mine for him. At any rate, he—and Dempsey and Dempsey's manager, Jack ("Doc") Kearns (who broke with the champion before the Tunney fight)—overlooked a historical lesson: Jim Corbett had been idle three years when Bob Fitzsimmons beat him. Jess Willard had been idle three years when Dempsey beat him. Jeffries had not fought in a long while before Corbett beat him. Ring rust can be the great leveler.

It was Rickard who was responsible, indirectly, for the fight being held in Pennsylvania instead of New York. The leading contender for the title was a big, sharp-boxing but slow-moving Negro heavyweight named Harry Wills, "The Brown Panther," but Rickard wouldn't promote a fight between Wills and Dempsey. He didn't appear to be bigoted, particularly; he just felt "mixed" fights didn't draw too well. The result was that the New York State Athletic Commission refused to allow Dempsey to appear in New York unless he boxed Wills.

So Dempsey had not put his title on the line since he had fought Firpo. Rickard's strategy worked from the crowd-appeal standpoint. By the fall of 1926 the country was overripe for a Big One. The newspapers, of course, were full of five, six, eight or ten stories a day from the training camps. The two fighters were, you must remember, the idols of the day. The psychologists had not yet loomed up with their calm theories that anyone who beat his breast and took mail-order lessons from

Charles Atlas or Lionel Strongfort to build up his muscles was, necessarily, a latent homosexual.

The crowds pushing their way into the training camps were tremendous. Tunney did most of his work in Stroudsburg, Pennsylvania, on the edge of the Glenbrook Country Club, and on a Sunday a week and a half before the bout, seven thousand persons jammed into the area, climbing trees, standing on grassy knolls and watching the not overly impressive challenger work studiously on perfecting his left jab. Another two thousand were turned away. Dempsey trained at Bader Field in Atlantic City, beset by assorted problems and lawsuits, and a little uneasy because, inside, he knew he was only a shadow of the fighter he had been. Tunney said of him, "He has lost that flaming impetuosity," and after Jack looked up the stilted phrase, he was inclined to agree. Tommy Loughran, the boxing master billed at the time as the uncrowned light-heavyweight champion, was his chief sparring partner, and on several days he made Dempsey look foolish. After one session, Dempsey said with his usual candor, "I was terrible. Tunney would have murdered me today."

Sportswriters who were called experts watched the Dempsey-Loughran sparring and observed that if Tunney were to win, he would do it with his right hand, because Dempsey seemed easy to hit with one—but they chose not to believe their eyes, and nearly all of them said the champion would knock out Tunney. Their stories helped make the titleholder a five-to-two favorite by ringtime. Only bluff, outspoken Harry Grayson of the NEA syndicate picked Tunney. Like Gene a former Marine, he had been on the West Coast earlier when Tunney was making a movie, *The Fighting Marine,* and had seen the challenger working out daily at the Hollywood Athletic Club. This was some six months before the fight and Grayson said flatly Dempsey would lose.

Psychology was in its professional infancy, but Tunney used a liberal dose of it on Dempsey before their first meeting in the ring. Most notably, on the day of the fight he flew from Stroudsburg to Philadelphia, an eighty-mile stretch, in a little plane piloted by stunt flier Casey Jones. This, in a day when only fools and daredevils took to the air.

Tunney says the flight was planned weeks before, with race driver Wade Morton making the arrangements. Grantland Rice told a different tale. As he saw it, Jones set his plane down on the golf course next to Stroudsburg and then urged the fighter to "come on up for a five-minute spin." Once they were airborne, the weather suddenly socked in the ground below and Jones blithely steered for Philadelphia and landed there in the thick, misty day, an hour and twenty minutes later.

Tunney's story seems a little more credible, if only because on the morning of the bout Rickard was standing in front of the Bellevue-Stratford Hotel in Philadelphia, talking with Billy Gibson, Gene's manager, and some sportswriters. Tex was leaning debonairly on his Malacca cane, pontificating, when one of the writers asked, "Hear the latest, Tex? We just got word that Tunney's flying into town for the weigh-in."

"Goddam that son of a bitch!" Rickard said. "What's he trying to do to me?"

Whereupon W. O. McGeehan, the New York writer, raised an eyebrow and said, "To you? What about himself?"

At any rate, Jones landed the plane at the Navy Flying

Field at 1:30 p.m., with Tunney pale and airsick. He was driven to the offices of the boxing commision, weighed in at 186½ and then went to the apartment of a friend to sleep and, later, eat a steak. Frank Weiner was chairman of the Pennsylvania boxing commission, and late in the afternoon at the home of sportsman Jules Mastbaum he said, "I've just weighed Tunney. I never saw anybody so scared. He is as white as a sheet. I hope he doesn't die of fright between now and ringtime."

Tunney's friend Bernard F. Gimbel, the merchant, was in the group at Mastbaum's house. He looked at Weiner. "Fright?" he asked. "Or illness?" He sighed. "Well, we'll see tonight."

Meanwhile Tunney slept a couple of hours, awoke and ate, went back to sleep until five o'clock—and was awakened this time by Billy Gibson, who arrived at the apartment with Max "Boo Boo" Hoff, the Philadelphia racketeer, and Hoff's lawyer. First Gibson asked Tunney to witness an agreement between Hoff and himself, which Gene did, and then he produced another document—the small print of which turned out to be a long-term agreement between Gibson and Tunney. Tunney even then was dissatisfied with some aspects of Gibson's behavior; he threw the papers at his manager and ordered him to leave. Later, after Tunney *did* fire him, Gibson was declared in court to be legally incompetent.

When Dempsey came by for the weigh-in, he wasn't sick, as Tunney was, but he wasn't in the best mental state. By this time he had broken with Kearns, but the old flimflam man wasn't letting him off the hook just like that. He fired a handful of court actions at the champion. demanding back salary. One day Estelle Taylor Dempsey, Jack's wife, was stopped while driving a car and had the automobile literally taken from under her because of a financial judgment. Almost always Dempsey's training camp had been a laugh-a-minute one, but not this time. There was an unfamiliar seriousness in the air. The aging killer of the ring had wealth, a beautiful wife and a revamped nose . . . but he had unhappiness.

TEX RICKARD liked to say, when impressed, "I ain't never seed anything like it," and that was the way it was when fight night arrived.

The confusion was almost total. Seventy thousand in the big crowd had come from the greater New York area, many of them by car, and the parking spaces weren't big enough and were far away from the arena. Fake tickets had been counterfeited, of course—standard procedure for a big sporting event—and there were sporadic arguments and fist fights over who belonged where. Everybody Who Was Anybody was there: Secretary of the Treasury Andrew W. Mellon, a half-dozen governors, countless mayors and Congressmen, Charles M. Schwab, Percy Rockefeller, Vincent Astor, Jimmy Walker, New York's "night mayor," William Randolph Hearst and Joseph Pulitzer, Anthony J. Drexel Biddle, Jr., W. Averell Harriman, Harry Payne Whitney, George and Joseph Widener. From show business, Tom Mix came into Philadelphia from Hollywood with his own special train and a party of five hundred. Charlie Chaplin, Norma Talmadge and Florenz Ziegfeld were also in the stands. Samuel Vauclain was on hand; the head of the Baldwin Locomotive Works was, in effect, the night's top bidder, since he had bought $27,000 worth of tickets for friends and associates. Peggy Hopkins Joyce sat in the third row, almost demure in a black dress and coat, except for a small bouquet of orchids (which would sag and collapse in the wet of the night) pinned to her lapel. Gertrude Ederle, who momentarily had replaced Marilyn Miller in the hearts of Americans, was with the moon-faced lawyer, Dudley Field Malone. Jack Kearns was flitting here and there, not bothering to confirm or deny the reports that he had bet $50,000 on Dempsey, his old meal ticket, despite the lawsuits he had flung at the champion.

Four thousand of Philadelphia's city policemen were on duty in and around the Sesquicentennial Stadium, in addition to the small army of ushers and special police who clustered around the ring, keeping order and breaking up heated discussions. The thirty-four arc lights over the ring threw a glare over the spectators, who looked a little washed out and waxen, even the show people. A clergyman or two may have been on the grounds, but Baptist, Methodist and Presbyterian ministers in Philadelphia were lying low and licking their wounds. They had tried unsuccessfully to have authorities stop the "low-down and degrading" contest between "two brutes." There were four hundred or more newsmen clustered around the ringside (if you paid $27.50 for a "ringside" seat, the chances were you were sixty rows back) and long before the main event they had started filing the two million words that would go out on the telegraph wires and set a record of its kind for sports-event coverage. The words would continue to go out sputteringly late that night as the downpour soaked the wires and short-circuited many of them, including the entire special layout installed by *The New York Times*. There even was a telegrapher on hand for the *Ocean Times,* the ship-news publication that was hurrying the events of the damp night out to a hundred liners at sea.

Tunney came to the arena early and sat in the ring for long minutes before Dempsey showed. The champion was so late, in fact, that when he did turn up at the dressing rooms, Rickard said worriedly, "Jack, for God's sake, hurry up. It's going to rain any minute."

There is an unwritten rule which nearly all fighters follow: predict ruin for an opponent. Dempsey, for all his brusque directness, was no exception. "Don't worry about the rain," he muttered at Rickard. "This guy ain't goin' over two rounds, anyway."

The air was thick with moisture, but it had not yet begun to rain when Dempsey pushed aside the top rope and climbed into the ring. He didn't have his usual two or three days' growth of beard—Philadelphia rules demanded the men be clean-shaven—and his body was different than, say, a half-dozen years before. Under the white sweater and the towel around his neck, it still was reasonably lean and (by man-in-the-street standards) superbly conditioned, but the ribs no longer were showing, the dark burn of the sun wasn't there . . . and some of the great, animal-like reflexes were not quite what they had been. "Jerry the Greek" Luvadis, his trainer, had Dempsey's old black-and-white-checked bathrobe over an arm.

Tunney got up, pulled his robe around him—blue with scarlet trim and a gold U.S. Marine emblem on the back —and walked over near the other. "Hello, Champion," he said, smiling.

Dempsey looked at him quickly. "Hello, Gene," he said.

"May the better man win," Tunney said, and Dempsey

looked a little startled. Perhaps the grammar floored him.

"Yeh, yeh," he said, and he turned back to Jerry, Gene Normile and Jack O'Brien. They bandaged his hands swiftly, while Tunney's seconds took their time wrapping the gauze on the challenger's hands.

The rain still had not come when referee Tommy Reilly, in white sweater and slacks, called the two men to the center of the ring for instructions. He warned Dempsey of rabbit-punching—that is, hitting chopping blows behind the ear—but the scowling titleholder seemed to pay him no heed. Years later Dempsey refereed a fight in which the classicist Loughran outboxed Max Baer. Back in the Warwick Hotel in Manhattan afterward, Jack showed Baer how he could have won. He hit Baer on the right biceps—this was when Dempsey was in his mid-thirties, but he left the flamboyant Max's arm useless for a half-hour—and then spun him around and hit him on the chin. "You can't do that," Baer protested, "it's illegal." Dempsey just looked at him disgustedly. "They'll only warn you the first time," he said.

THEN THE FIGHT began, with the thousands on thousands of fans roaring from the opening bell in the damp darkness. For a little, they had to live on their anticipation, because the two boxers did virtually nothing.

They moved around, shuffled in and out, pawed at each other. Dempsey threw a quick left hook, but it missed and Tunney clinched. Again the same pattern. Tunney feinted with a left of his own and Dempsey blinked. Dempsey missed another left hook—and Tunney, ever the diagnostician, saw something. He noticed that when Jack hooked, he took an "extra hitch" to get a bit more length and leverage to the punch. It wasn't much, just a brief hesitation, the way a baseball hitter may cock his bat with a little jiggle before swinging . . . but it took extra time.

The next left Dempsey tried, Tunney stepped in and hit him with a straight, hard right on the cheekbone— and won the fight.

Ah, it's a little too high for the knockout, Tunney thought, but the shot staggered Dempsey; he sagged a little in his tracks and moved in for the clinch. For the rest of the round he kept Tunney tied up, using all the years, all the fights, all the experience, to do this, while he tried to clear his head. When he got back to his corner at round's end, he breathed deeply from the smelling salts that Jerry the Greek held up to him. Still shaken, dizzy, he tried to keep the challenger, sitting across the ring, from seeing how groggy he was. Most of the newsmen were fooled. Only a few of them, dictating their stories to the telegraphers, said that Dempsey barely had weathered the round, but that was the way it was. "Jerry gave me the smelling salts," Dempsey was to say later, "but it was my legs that needed help. The salts didn't help there. I sat there in my corner and thought, 'I'm an old man.' "

After that, the fight was one-sided and a little dreary. Tunney raked the champion's face and body with his Corbett-like straight rights and lefts, kept away from Dempsey's desperate punches, and drubbed him. Now and then Gene glanced over the ropes and grinned at Mike Trant, a Chicago policeman who had been the champion's bodyguard and kept yelling, "Come on, Jack! Knock the big sissy into my lap!" But in command of the fight as he was, he never took any chances. He piled up points with his boxing, but he never seemed to feel the taste of blood and go out and try to finish off Dempsey.

Possibly that was why the crowd didn't warm to him as he went about his methodical task. The blood lust, to use an old saw, is a big part of a fight mob's make-up—was it in S. N. Behrman's *No Time for Comedy* that a character said, "Let's face it; the average man is bloodthirsty and contemptible"?—and for the mob, the name of the game is savagery. There was none in Tunney. To him, it still was the manly art of self-defense.

(In 1925, in a room atop the Putnam Building in mid-New York, he had boxed three two-minute rounds for a movie short with the fifty-nine-year-old Corbett, his early idol. Dressed in long whites, the still handsome Corbett had the remnants of his great left feints and hooks, and after he and the young Tunney had sparred the three rounds, Tunney said, "I honestly think he's better than Benny Leonard. It was the greatest thing I've ever seen in the ring.")

The rain came down, lightly at first and then steadily, soakingly, beginning in the fourth round. Dempsey became bloodier and weaker, shuffling after the elusive challenger, and only in the sixth did he land well. He threw a wild left hook and it caught Tunney on the Adam's apple —so hard that for days Gene was to be hoarse and cough up blood.

But the fight went on dully to the end of the ten rounds and the noises of the great crowd grew fainter and fainter. They knew what they were seeing and they kept hoping with each round that the sequence of events would change—but they knew it wouldn't. When the last bell clanged, there was almost total silence. They looked at the man from Colorado, swaying and battered in mid-ring, and they believed what they saw . . . but they didn't want to.

FOR THE MOMENT, the big story was over. The soaked crowd, the milling thousands, filed out feeling empty and disappointed. The story hadn't gone the way they had expected—but then, tomorrow was another day and in 1926 there always were big stories.

Not war stories, not tales of diplomatic green baize tables—but, rather, big events involving single people. Just the month before, Commander Richard Evelyn Byrd had flown over the North Pole, which no one else had done, and had come back to a welcome in Wall Street from 50,000 New Yorkers. Gertrude Ederle had Ameri-can-crawled her way across the English Channel, and the papers had trumpeted TRUDY DOES IT! Rudolph Valen-tino had died, and 30,000 cosmopolites, who were sup-posed to be blasé about such things, had stormed Frank E. Campbell's Memorial Chapel in Manhattan to see the Sheik himself laid out in immaculate evening dress. Earl Carroll had just been arrested for breaking the Prohibi-tion law; he had given a party at his *Vanities* theater during which a nude showgirl named Joyce Hawley had splashed around in a tub full of champagne from which the guests drank. A free-swinging tabloid newspaper, the New York *Mirror,* had reopened a four-year-old murder case involving people called Hall and Mills, and Babe Ruth was ending another big year. He would be signing a three-year contract for $210,000 with the Yankees be-fore the next season began.

There were always big stories, then—but here, this wretched night, the curtain just had rung down on this one. The actors still were there. Particularly the lean, dark, muscular man with the short haircut, William Harrison Dempsey. He stood there now in the brightness of the ring, the rain slanting across the lights, and he couldn't see. His face was bruised and cut and his eyes were almost closed. He felt old and sick to his stomach and he wanted to get away from there, out of the cold late-summer rain—anyplace, as long as it was away. He stood in his corner, unsteady, and then he reached up and groped for an old-time fighter named Philadelphia Jack O'Brien, a pug from another day who was one of his seconds. He grabbed O'Brien's arm, and the words he said came out thickly and almost incoherently.

"Take me to him," he muttered. "Take me to him."

O'Brien put an arm around him and so did Normile, his nominal manager, and Jerry the Greek. They shepherded the beaten, bloody man slowly across the ring to where Gene Tunney stood, the new heavyweight boxing champion of the world, trying to shrug his damp bathrobe over his head to keep off the rain, trying to take in what had happened and to understand what it meant, shaking this hand and that, smiling and trying to be polite to everyone.

Dempsey put up his hand feebly and slapped Tunney on the back, but it was more of a clinging than a slap. "All right, Gene," he said painfully, slowly. "All right, good luck." The square-jawed, pompadoured Tunney's face softened—*I can see myself the way he is now,* he thought; *I can see myself going over to someone else and trying to get out the words*—and he said thanks. Dempsey turned and the three men helped him through the ropes and out of the ring and down the few steps and up the aisle to the dressing room.

In the wetness, in the foulness of the night, the thousands stopped and turned and watched him vanish with his few faithful around him.

Then they started yelling. They seemed to forget their own discomfort and they shouted his name . . . and the bloody, pain-racked man heard it, just a little before he got under the shelter of the stadium and into the dressing room. If he could have smiled, he would have. *Now they love me,* Jack Dempsey thought, and because he was a man who liked to laugh, he tried to then, but it was too hard to manage.

An hour or so later most of the people had cleared out of the stadium and were trying to get a conveyance back to town—there simply were none—and Dempsey came out with a few of his handlers and they got into a car and drove back through the teeming night to a hotel in the center of Philadelphia. They went through the lobby, and little knots of people stared and pointed and said there he goes, and when he got upstairs, he limped slowly into the bedroom, eased himself to the edge of the bed . . . and, covering his face with his aching hands, began to sob. Only for a little while. Then he wiped the tears dry, this man to whom crying didn't come easily, and he swung his exhausted body slowly onto the bed and stretched out. For a half-hour Jerry the Greek gave him a slow, careful rubdown; then Dempsey turned over and fell asleep.

At just about that moment, his wife—the dark-eyed, exotic, moderately successful movie actress Estelle Taylor, whose prettiness was so often masked by the almost grotesque make-up of the screen siren—was getting a breath of Indiana air while waiting for the Pennsylvania Limited to pull out of Fort Wayne. She heard the news-boys on the station platform yelling the story of his defeat, but her mind was on the next day, when she would be at the Philadelphia hotel with him (Dempsey felt wives shouldn't see their husbands fight) and he would put his arms around her and reach up and tousle her dark hair.

THAT WAS THE way it ended, in the blood, the mud and the rain in suburban Philadelphia. In the hours past midnight, Dempsey slept his worn, sad sleep and Tunney sat up for a while in a small hotel in Philadelphia, sipping tea and talking with a few friends, and then he, too, went soundly to asleep. The next day Dempsey was to meet his wife and joke a little and feel better, and he would say that he wanted a return match. But a few days later a delayed reaction set in and he remembered the way Tun-ney had walked out and hit him in the first round, the way his legs had come apart at the seams, the way he suddenly had become an old man. To Tex Rickard first and then to the world at large, Dempsey spoke his mind: he would quit. He was finished with boxing. "I've had it," the big man from Colorado said, and there it was.

Or was it?

CHAPTER 2

IT WAS THE strangest of times, made more so by the curious fact that it was not only the young who fashioned it.

Somehow the young always seem to rearrange the world—or at least its outward appearance. In the middle Sixties, young men wore long hair and tight pants; the young women had long, stringy, unbrushed hair and dresses even higher over the knees than in the Twenties . . . and here and there, a handful of the older ones fell in line. It was the young men who began with padded shoulders and draped jackets in the Thirties and the young women who started wearing the feathered Empress Eugénie hats . . . and soon everyone was.

But the Twenties were different and peculiar. It wasn't

25

only the sixteen- and eighteen-year-olds. It was the day of the sheik and the flapper—but there were thirty, forty and even sixty-year-old sheiks and flappers.

It was as if the great barrier reef between the ages, the one that so flatly refuses to let the young and the old and the middle-aged come together on any campground where they might have a faint chance of understanding what the other is up to, suddenly had collapsed. Poof, just like that, everyone was of an age. Old, young, medium—there was no differential. The United States of America was a houseparty, a whoop-de-do weekend in Bronxville or Carmel or Grosse Pointe, and all were invited.

If something was good, it was nifty or the nuts. Total elation came with "Hot dog!" You brushed off someone with "Go fly a kite," and the password of the cynic was "It's the bunk." People sang Irving Berlin songs and "Bye, Bye, Blackbird," and a wild night at home included listening to the A. & P. Gypsies or the Happiness Boys, Billy Jones and Ernie Hare, on the radio.

Americans went blind from bathtub gin, and Sunday mornings on the country-club porch were devoted to weak cries of "My God, was I *drunk* last night!" Liquor was called booze and hooch, and there was no way of knowing that forty years later, camp-style, the terms would be resurrected.

The magazines you read were *Life,* a funny one edited by a tall man named Robert E. Sherwood (even then working on his play *The Road to Rome*), and *Judge* and *College Humor,* to which you turned impatiently for the latest Kay Brush story. The sleek, wry Miss Brush was a true historian of the times; at one point she even had seven different-colored typewriters, one for each day of the week, which seemed logical for the setting of—did she or Scott Fitzgerald first call it the Jazz Age? No matter.

The American newspaper still was passably sedate, but in Manhattan, Bernarr MacFadden, of all people—he was a physical-culturist who walked briskly, ate nuts and fruit and called almost belligerently for the clean life— had spawned a grotesque something with tinted pages, the tabloid *Graphic,* with a gossip columnist named Winchell and a young sportswriter named Ed Sullivan. It didn't last long and no one but its founder took it seriously, but ah, my friends and oh, my foes, it gave a bizarre light.

Nobody really knew the names of politicians, of course. Why should they? What had they done lately? Oh, there were chuckles and rumbles from a dark, round little man named Fiorello La Guardia who was a Representative from New York State, but generally it was a rare American who knew the name of his Congressman.

In the movies you watched Ben Lyon, Reginald Denny, Richard Dix, Douglas Fairbanks, Vilma Banky, Garbo, Clara Bow from Bay Ridge, Brooklyn, and Lois Wilson. If you were male, you became irked at the way your woman's breasts heaved as she watched Ronald Colman in *Beau Geste.* If you danced—the Charleston, what else?—it was to Paul Whiteman's huge mishmash of a "jazz band" or Ben Bernie's orchestra or Vincent Lopez'.

You drove a Willys-Knight or a Hupmobile, a Marmon or a Locomobile, or, if you were affluent, a Pierce-Arrow. Everyone—there were no exceptions, not even

27

trolley motormen—was in the stock market, and on the playing fields of Yankee Stadium and Forest Hills and Madison Square Garden there had evolved a race of giants. Pudgy, raspy, jovially vulgar Babe Ruth, who swung a baseball bat. Mincing William Tatum Tilden, a homosexual who swung a tennis racquet as it never had been swung before. Young Robert Tyre Jones and older Walter Hagen, who swung golf clubs. There was Notre Dame and its Knute Rockne, the first of the university football factories and foremen, and the glum Helen Wills, unbeatable from the baseline in tennis and called "Little Miss Poker Face" by Mr. Sullivan, the young sportswriter. And, whirling around the edges, the madhouse called the six-day bicycle race.

There they were, then, the names of cars and people and places and songs and dances, just as now—but with one singular difference. It was *all* fun and games. Every woman was Queen Marie of Rumania, every man the Prince of Wales falling from a horse, breaking his collarbone and laughing about it. Maybe that was it. The world was laughing so hard about everything. There was another universe outside, of course; China was hissing and erupting, with heads rolling—or, more specifically, being impaled on poles—and in Rome, Benito Mussolini was a comic-opera figure with his belly bulge and jutting underlip. But no one Out There laughed. No one laughed much anywhere, really, except from Maine to California. Inside that compound, it was almost hysterical.

ON FRIDAY, September 24, 1926, there was just a smell of winter in the land.

In New York the temperature was in the upper seventies and people talked of Indian summer, although there had been no first frost. Already the light early-autumn storms had dusted the Rockies. Soon some of the passes would be closed and the winds would strip the bushes and trees near the bases of the mountains. There were snow flurries in Evanston, just outside Chicago.

In San Francisco a man named Harry Melosh was arrested. He had told police that the kidnaping of the evangelist Aimee Semple McPherson was a hoax, that she had spent ten days in a Carmel, California, cottage with her former radio operator and that he, Melosh, had had a hand in the project.

From George Palmer Putnam's Arctic expedition, word came back that an Eskimo convert to Christianity had confessed killing Ross Marvin, Admiral Peary's right-hand man, who had been sent back from near the North Pole by the Admiral sixteen years before. Marvin had been believed drowned.

The St. Louis Cardinals beat the New York Giants, 6 to 4, and clinched the National League baseball title. It was, naturally, the most vital news, front-page everywhere. On Broadway, Marilyn Miller was playing in *Sunny,* Florence Reed in *The Shanghai Gesture* and Eddie Dowling in *Honeymoon Lane.* Jeanne Eagels was touring in *Rain.*

In the movies John Barrymore was Don Juan, and many people in many country clubs in the suburbs poured passable whiskey from bottles in paper bags on Saturday night and discussed the picture intellectually, although the customer lines were somewhat longer for Mary Pickford in *Sparrows* and Harold Lloyd in *For Heaven's Sake.*

It was warm and muggy in Philadelphia, which seemed to be coming slowly out of a hangover. There was a report that the Bellevue-Stratford valet had pressed 687 suits. The Ritz-Carlton claimed almost the same number, but both claims, possibly, were apocryphal.

TUNNEY AWAKENED late in the morning. That alone made it an unusual day for him. The year around, he was an early riser, even during the long stretches when he was not in serious training. But it had been a long night, and after he had come back to the hotel, he had stayed up for some time.

There was no special tiredness, no aching in his beautifully conditioned body. He hadn't been hit that much except for one hard punch in the throat. He talked with friends and they smiled and were relaxed. Billy Gibson, his manager, came by in a golf suit with plus-four knickerbockers and he was the noisiest of all, the words spilling out happily. Gibson had had other fighters, and some of them had been good ones. It had been unlikely that he ever would have another one, for example, such as Benny Leonard, the lightweight champion who could do it all in the ring. But this time he had gotten his hands on the big one, the great magoo, the only one that meant much not only to prizefight buffs but, generally, to everyone.

During the talk, people kept saying to Tunney, well, you're the champ now, and he grinned and nodded. He didn't pinch himself or rub his eyes. He had known the night before—long rounds before the last bell. He was not a golly-gee-whiz man.

He breakfasted and dressed in a blue serge suit, looking at the big, almost square image in the full-length mirror, seeing the serious, almost handsome face with the blue eyes and the light brown hair. It was not, all in all, a fighter's face. No cauliflower ears, no broken nose. Slim it a bit at the sides and darken the hair and it might have been James J. Corbett.

That thought would have pleased Tunney. He was so like Corbett, thoughtful, logical, precise. A boxer, not a fighter. Either of them could use the phrase "the manly art of self-defense" and it wouldn't sound incongruous. He touched his lips lightly; they were just the faintest bit swollen. There was a slight cut over his left eye, but a strip of sticking plaster had taken care of that.

Usually he went hatless, but now he put on a light brown felt fedora and he and Gibson went over to Tex Rickard's suite at the Bellevue-Stratford.

The newsmen had come alive by this time and some of them were in the lobby with Doc Kearns, who was talking as usual.

The Doctor, dressed as always like a Broadway mobster, was pacing around and joking and he sounded as if he meant it, although no one really knew why. He had been suing Dempsey, but reportedly had bet somewhere between $50,000 and $100,000 on Jack. Years had gone and many things had happened since he had started whittling Dempsey into the man he had become, and he no longer managed the fighter. There was no real bitterness, despite the lawsuits. The two of them had made a great deal of money, and Kearns had sliced a big chunk of it off the top. He still liked Jack. The lawyer stuff was strictly business.

"I guess the laugh is on me," he said to the sportswriters, waving his hands in a palms-upward gesture. "That

31

is, if anyone can scare up a laugh around here this morning."

Upstairs, Tex Rickard, his gold-headed cane off in a corner, was in his shirt sleeves, expansive and pleased. His man had lost, but otherwise God was in His heaven. Tunney shook hands with him.

"How is Jack this morning?" he asked.

Rickard shrugged. "Hurting. That's only natural. He'll be all right."

They talked for just a little while, and then Tunney went to luncheon with former Governor James M. Cox of Ohio and Dan Hanna, the Cleveland newspaper owner. Gibson stayed behind. It was touch and go whether he talked more upstairs than Kearns did downstairs.

THE PHILADELPHIA papers, of course, were on the stands by now, and the people who had seen the fight or heard Graham McNamee describe it on the radio bought them up quickly and sat back to read what they had seen or heard.

Hardheaded Philadelphia businessmen made rough calculations and told reporters the bout had brought nearly $5,000,000 in trade to the city. It was duly noted.

In California a wire-service reporter telephoned to Glendale to old Jess Willard, who seven years before had lost the championship to Dempsey at Maumee Bay in Toledo. "It's the same old story," Willard said. "A champion can stay at the top only so long."

Over the telegraph wires across the Atlantic came the news that a Major Wilson, who promoted fights in England, had made the first offer for a return bout, proposing

Wembley Stadium in London, which seated 150,000.

For weeks, months, years, readers of *The New York Times* had read in Jim Dawson's fight stories on the sports pages that there was only one Goliath and his name was Dempsey. This Friday they were a little startled to read: "In defeat, Dempsey was revealed as an overrated fighter, a man who was good but never great." Mr. Dawson was most expert at flip-flopping; in the months to come, there would be more of the same. Of course, he was not alone among sportswriters, but it must be remembered that America was in a period when these occasionally seedy bravos were considered crosses between Nostradamus and Henry James.

By FIVE O'CLOCK the mugginess had cleared away and it was a good late-summer day in Philadelphia. Estelle Taylor arrived at the Adelphi Hotel after her long train trip and immediately took the elevator to the sixth floor. Her husband met her at the door. He was up and about by now.

The area around his left eye was discolored and shut tight, and there was a cut under his right eye. Six stitches had been taken in the cut over his left eye. The new nose, however—the actor's nose—had come out of it all right. Sleep during the night had been hard to come by, what with the pain, and it had been fitful; but there were pills in him by this time and the sharpest of the aches that had come in waves through the dark hours were gone. There was only stiffness, soreness and a kind of weakness. It wasn't all that new to him. Dempsey had been fighting since he was eleven, which made twenty years, and he had known this kind of morning—and worse—before.

It was just that not many people remembered he had. Deities' misdemeanors of the past have a way of being mislaid.

There still were people in his suite. Sportswriters, hangers-on, Jerry the Greek, Gene Normile, Gus Wilson. Dempsey grinned lopsidedly at Estelle and put his arms around her and he could feel her beginning to sob as he held her. Theirs hadn't been the smoothest of marriages and even now it was beginning to ravel a little, but she loved him. The tears coming down her face, she pushed him away a little and asked what happened.

"Honey," he said, and it was a little painful to smile, but he did, "I just forgot to duck."

One of the newsmen heard it. When it got into the papers the next day, it was to change abruptly the relationship between Jack Dempsey and the fluctuating public of the United States. Before, the populace had liberally booed him, plagued him, muttered that he had been a war slacker and prayed that the men he had fought—amiable Bill Brennan, skillful Tommy Gibbons, the fierce larger-than-life Luis Angel Firpo—would knock his block off. Now suddenly the old lion had lost his hold on the pride, and the people read what he had said to his wife at the door of the Adelphi room and said, You know, I guess he's really not a bad guy at that.

IN THE EARLY evening Tunney came to Dempsey's room and stayed briefly after shaking hands. Like most professional fighters, they had no anger toward each other. They tried to kill in the ring, Dempsey in particular, but to them that was all part of the work and, as the saying had it, all the rest was talk.

When Tunney was leaving, Dempsey touched him
lightly on the arm. "Steer clear of fakers and fair-weather
friends, Gene," he said. Gene nodded. They both knew
the advice really wasn't necessary.

The sportswriters on the afternoon papers now had
done their "recap" stories, and some of them dealt with
the men waiting in the wings for the new champion.
There were a couple of good trial horses—Harry Persson
from Sweden and a big Midwesterner named Monte
Munn. Jack Delaney, the fancy-dancing light-heavyweight champion. Jack Sharkey, a onetime sailor who
had come along quickly. The biggest name in the bunch
was that of Harry Wills, the Negro heavyweight who for
several years had been deprived of a shot at the title.
There seemed no prospect that Tunney suddenly would
single him out and give him a chance at the title now.

All through the day and stretching into the night, the
great exodus from Philadelphia had gone on. The estimated 70,000 New Yorkers who had crowded into the
city ninety miles away for the bout, found it harder to get
out than to get in. The first batch had made it back to
Manhattan by 1:30 a.m. the night of the fight, but it
took sixty-eight special trains and any number of regu-
larly scheduled ones to get all the rest back. The other
passengers on the regular trains looked at the ones getting on in Philadelphia, studied their mud-covered shoes
and shapeless clothes, and wondered.

The crush of the homeward-bound was no respecter of
persons. Billy Gibson, still in his sharp golf outfit, found
himself a seat in a parlor car, but Doc Kearns, out of the
money again, had to go by day coach. Rickard left in the
afternoon, and when he reached New York, reporters

buttonholed him in his Madison Square Garden office. "I was sorry to see Dempsey lose," he said. "Jack has been a fine boy. There has never been anything like this before, but I am not ready to say there never again will be anything like it."

The reporters knew Rickard well. Seven-league boots. They understood, naturally, that he never would be ready to say there wouldn't again be anything like it.

ON SATURDAY, the twenty-fifth of September, the two men headed in different directions. Dempsey and his Estelle went down to Atlantic City, still warm and with a soft sea breeze although the season was past, while Tunney entrained for New York. He almost didn't, actually. Hurrying to make the train connection, the cab carrying him swung wide around City Hall Plaza, skidded twenty feet and almost rammed into a trolley. Tunney took it with a patient grin.

There was no ticker-tape parade for him back in Manhattan, even though by this time the city seemed to be staging such shows at least semimonthly for assorted aviators and English Channel swimmers—but his welcome came close to being a demonstration. Thousands of New Yorkers pushed and shoved and poked their way through Pennsylvania Station to see the new champion, and they almost swept Tunney along with them as he made his way with a police escort to the Thirty-first Street exit of the station. Official municipal limousines took him and his entourage down Seventh Avenue on the way to City Hall, and again the streets were jammed with cheering people.

At the Hall, Tunney was spirited into the quarters of

the Board of Estimate, where he shook hands with and was greeted warmly by Mayor Walker. Grover (The Greeter) Whalen, the city's official host, was on hand with his ever-present boutonnière, and so, too, was Colonel John J. Phelan of the 165th Infantry, who was described to curious newsmen as "chief of the Mayor's military staff." Outside City Hall there was another crowd of well-wishers and Tunney spoke briefly to them and waved, explaining that one of Dempsey's punches had left him too hoarse to make a speech.

It was back uptown to the Biltmore then; in the limousine, Tunney chuckled at Walker's description of the Philadelphia bout: "The greatest swimming exhibition I have ever witnessed." The Biltmore, hard by Grand Central Terminal and even then famous for its lobby clock under which Princeton freshmen met Smith girls, seemed appropriate for Gene. It was one of the upper-crust commercial hotels in New York, just down the block from the Yale Club, and as Tunney strode to the elevators, he seemed as much at home as any Ivy Leaguer. Greenwich Village and the rough-and-ready days already seemed to be fading swiftly.

Upstairs, he held brief court for the sportswriters, and once again the atmosphere seemed to fall immediately into the easiness, the old-shoe comfort, of fight talk. Billy Gibson was there, his golf knickers replaced by city garb now, and he chewed out some of the writers who had made excuses for Dempsey after the fight. "Dempsey the best day he ever saw could not lick Gene Tunney," Gibson snorted. Tunney listened patiently. He was used to his excitable manager sounding off.

"I think Billy is a little bit too tough on the writers he's

37

talking about," he said, choosing his words carefully. "But then, I guess I've always baffled them. They always made me a short-ender"—he smiled—"and I'm grateful on behalf of the boys in the Village. They have profited handsomely in the betting.

"I do think Dempsey has been treated badly. I don't think he was treated fairly in respect to his actions when the war was on. There were many who didn't get into it and had no more excuse than Dempsey."

Over at the Garden, Rickard began to think about the next fight. One thing was certain, he told those reporters who had trailed him there: Harry Wills wasn't going to get a shot at the title. Not, Rickard explained, because he was anti-Negro, but, rather, because of Paddy Mullins, his manager.

"There's no room for such as him in sport," Tex said. "He tried to say he was offered a bout with Tunney last year only on condition that his fighter lay down."

Late in the afternoon Tunney went up to his mother's house on Arlington Avenue in the Riverdale section of Manhattan, the reporters dispersed and New York got down to the serious business of spending the customary wild Saturday night awash in bootleg liquor. No city could get more excited about a big fight or a new champion than New York, but when the moment was done, that was it and there were other items to attend to. The phrase, specifically, was "making whoopee."

CHAPTER 3

In 1926 the state of Connecticut still was considered more or less a social compound; it had not yet given ground readily to the middle-income crowd, the junior executives and so on. It seemed almost incongruous that Gene Tunney went there to spend the first weekend after the title fight. He was the guest of Samuel F. Prior in Field Point Park, had luncheon at the home of Mrs. George Lauder, Jr., in Rockridge—Mrs. Lauder had a pretty, brown-haired daughter named Polly—and played some golf at the Greenwich Country Club before heading finally for the huge, rococo, almost absurdly luxurious Westchester-Biltmore, later to be called the Westchester Country Club. Even the names—Field Point Park, Prior, Lauder, Greenwich—somehow seemed out of joint for a prizefighter. And *golf?*

But slowly, a little uncertainly, America was starting

to realize it had a rather uncommon man as its new heavyweight champion.

Heavyweight *boxing* champion. Mr. Tunney liked that word, boxing.

West Fifty-second Street in Manhattan, where he was born—in an apartment over a grocery store at number 414—was later to degenerate into a riverside slum, but then it was just a rough-and-ready neighborhood filled with working people who spent Saturday nights at the corner saloon and Sunday mornings repenting at Mass. Tunney's father was a stevedore named John, who had been born in the Village and had moved uptown after he married Mary Landon from Castle Bar, County Mayo. They had seven children, ultimately, three boys and four girls, and James Joseph Tunney, who was to be called Gene, was born to them on May 25, 1897.

The other boys were John, who was to die in an auto accident, and Tom, who became a detective, and the girls grew up as Rose, Margaret, Agnes and Sister Mary Assumpta. The Tunneys got no priest from their family, as devout Catholic parents so often hope, but they did get a Dominican nun.

James Joseph was called Gene early in his boyhood. He grew up tall and skinny—for, like so many Irishmen, he was to develop late—and he was quieter and more reserved than most of the boys in the neighborhood. Which didn't mean he particularly went out of his way to avoid the street fights that sprang up in Irish neighborhoods like so many hourly geysers.

John Tunney was a fight fan, almost a rabid one. When he could make the time, he went down to Owney Geaghan's boxing club on the Bowery, where John L. Sullivan had fought when he first came to New York

City, and where John Tunney had even had a bout himself. He took on the house professional and wasn't dis-
graced in losing, but when he looked at himself in the
mirror the next morning, he had two fine, lusty black
eyes.

When Gene was five months old, the Tunneys moved
back to the Village, and nine and a half years later, on
Gene's tenth birthday, he got a present: boxing gloves.
"You look the most likely," his father said thoughtfully,
although wondering a little about the boy's skinniness.
Even then, however, Gene was building the foundation.
As he went into the teen years, he played handball and
basketball, he swam, he ran and he jumped. And, of
course, there was school at Saint Veronica's, a good
parochial institution.

The day he got the boxing gloves was memorable. He
fought his brothers and four or five companions until
every nose was swollen, every set of lips bruised. They
kept up the daily "bouts" until the gloves actually fell
apart. And always, of course, there were the street fights.
One lasted three days, starting in front of the White Star
Line pier and being continued daily after school.

With each passing month, however, Gene fought less
and less in the street. He looked toward the professional
ring. And, as was only natural, he acquired an idol: Jack
Goodman, a skillful West Side lightweight who lived in
the same block—Perry Street—as the Tunneys. The
sportswriters called him "Handsome Jack, the Idol of the
West Side," and Gene would wait outside his door and
follow him through the streets.

AT FIFTEEN, schooling stopped for Tunney and he went
to work as an office boy, at five dollars a week, for the

41

Ocean Steamship Company. Even then, apparently, he felt there was a right way and a wrong way to do things. His job application to the company ended with "and, dear sir, believe me to be your most obedient servant," which in those days was the right way.

There was work, then, but still there was boxing. At sixteen, he helped a young beginning boxer named Willie Ward to train—first in the back of Dave Bernstein's drugstore and later at the Villagers' Athletic Club—and soon he was fighting three-round bouts at smokers, such as those held at the Knights of Columbus Council Hall at Twenty-third Street and Second Avenue. There was no pay, no gold watch to be bought back by the promoter for twenty dollars. He fought for ginger ale and a ham sandwich.

Years later Sinclair Lewis was to tell an interviewer: "It's nice to be paid to write. I was going to do it anyway."

At eighteen, Gene fought his first professional bout at the Sharkey Athletic Club, a dingy loft on Lincoln Square. He fought a boy named Bobby Dawson, considerably more experienced, and Dawson, knocked down for a nine count in the seventh round, didn't come out for the eighth. Tunney got $18 for the bout and was on his way.

He continued pro boxing in and around New York for several years—also working his way up to $17 a week at the Ocean Steamship Company as a rate clerk. When war was declared with Germany on April 6, 1917, Tunney tried to join the Marines, but a basketball injury to his left elbow caused his rejection. For more than a year, first quitting his job and working as a lifeguard at Keansburg,

New Jersey, and later taking long months of diathermy treatments from Dr. Frederick de Kraft of West Seventieth Street, he sweated to overcome the injury—Dr. de Kraft diagnosed it as a traumatic neuritis—and in June of 1918 he was accepted by the Marines.

THERE WERE 2,500,000 American soldiers, sailors and Marines overseas in those years, and comparatively few of them saw action. Until he began to build a reputation as a boxer in the service, Tunney's toughest moments in Europe were guarding empty balloon sheds and airplane hangars, two hours on and four off, twenty-four on and twenty-four off.

But the young Irish body was still growing. He got up to 168 pounds, making him a rather light light-heavyweight, and after some local successes he entered the AEF tournament. The finals were held at the Cirque de Paris and Tunney fought twice. With a still-broken knuckle on his right hand from a previous bout in Tours— and a good right hand is almost vital to beat a left-hander, since with it you slip inside left swings—he first fought an Allentown, Pennsylvania, southpaw named K. O. Sullivan (who already had fought Jack Dillon and Battling Levinsky professionally) and won a ten-round decision.

In the final bout Tunney met Ted Jamison, the American amateur light-heavyweight champion, and there was no question this time of favoring the right hand. Tunney threw it time and again, putting the pain behind him, and he won.

After that, there were exhibitions to be fought in the Rhineland—it was late spring of 1919 by now—and once, on a Rhine boat going from Coblenz to Cologne, he talked with a Marine, a former newsman from Missouri named McReynolds, about the man named Dempsey who just had been matched with Jess Willard for the heavyweight championship.

Tunney smiled, half to himself. "The question is," he said aloud, "will Gene Tunney, the clever boxer, ever defeat Jack Dempsey, the rugged fighter?" McReynolds grinned at him. "You're young," he said. "You're fast, you're clever. You can take it. It ought to be possible for you to do that someday."

"I will," Tunney said.

IT WAS THERE, on the boat on the Rhine, then, that he made up his mind. He would be a professional boxer by trade, for better or worse.

In the last months of his European tour, he met Eddie Eagan, the onetime Yale scholar who had won the American college and amateur heavyweight titles before entering the service. "When you get back home," Eagan said to Tunney in July of 1919, "why don't you come to Yale with me?"

"I won't have any time," Gene said. "I'm going to win the heavyweight championship of the world." Eagan, who had admired Dempsey for a long time and was aware that Jack had knocked out Willard for the title ten days before, almost laughed. Tunney seemed so grave. But Eagan didn't quite laugh.

Tunney came home to Greenwich Village with a $60 discharge bonus in his pocket; a suit, a hat and shoes ate up all of that. For a month he relaxed, and then he began work at his chosen trade in earnest.

44

It took nearly six months to get started, to find some-body to fight. An opponent finally turned up in Dan O'Dowd, a Boston heavyweight who just had fought an eight-round no-decision bout with Bill Brennan, one of the top-ranking contenders for Dempsey's title. Tunney faced him on December 15, 1919, at the Bayonne Athletic Association, which was a euphemism for a cold, heatless shed in an amusement park in New Jersey. Gene won and collected $201. His then manager, Billy Roche, took his cut and Tunney was left with $150.75 . . . in ones, fives and twos.

He took it home to Perry Street and, at breakfast the next morning, dumped it onto the table in the dining room. Mary Landon Tunney's eyes widened. "God bless and spare the hands that can make so much money in one night," she exclaimed. But a couple of days later she was prodding him to get into a "gentlemanly" business. He almost had. Just before getting the bout with O'Dowd, he had phoned the Ocean Steamship Company and made an oblique inquiry about getting back his old job. There was no opening.

THERE WERE seven years of it, after that. It was a little longer than standard for a prizefighter at the time to reach the top, but not that much longer. What you did was fight one trial horse after another, in small fight clubs that kept getting a bit larger each time around, and from each of them you learned something.

Always, Tunney learned something.

For instance, he fought one Whitey Allen of the Bronx at the Jersey City Armory on New Year's Day. For days Tunney meditated and puzzled and worried about Allen's right hand, supposedly fearsome. When the fight started, Allen rushed out and threw his bomb—and Tunney dropped his head under it and jammed a short left uppercut into Allen's stomach. For a round and a half Allen tossed rights and Tunney ducked them and scored with lefts, and midway in the second Gene let go his first straight right and knocked the other out. Tunney had learned one more item about his strange business: don't worry before a fight. Excepting the nightmare he had before the first Dempsey fight, he almost never worried again.

When Tunney fought Soldier Jones in the semifinal bout to the Dempsey-Carpentier event on July 2, 1921, he was heavy and sluggish. He had spent a good deal of the spring and early summer in Canada and Maine, chopping trees and working as a laborer to strengthen his injury-riddled hands. The heavy duty had left him fourteen pounds heavier, at 189, and he wasn't particularly proud of his seventh-round technical knockout of Jones.

An unimpressive fight, then. All fighters have them. But it's doubtful any one of the 90,000 in attendance would have come out flatly and said that the Tunney of that fight would defeat both of the stars of the main bout. Which, of course, he did.

John Tunney never came to see his son fight. True, he loved boxing and he *did* give Gene the boxing gloves when he was ten, but he lived until 1923 without having seen the younger Tunney in the ring. "Do you think I would be happy seeing you bleeding?" he said once to his son. And, having second thoughts, "You take your mother's and my advice and do not do this thing any more."

Uphill then, slowly. The first time he appeared in

46

Madison Square Garden, he won a technical knockout over Jack Burke of Pittsburgh . . . with Jack Dempsey among the spectators. In 1922 he decisioned Battling Levinsky and became the American light-heavyweight champion, a position that Rickard thoughtfully had resurrected from the mothballs.

Four months later Tunney fought Harry Greb, who had one of the more picturesque nicknames of a picturesque time: "The Pittsburgh Windmill." It fitted him. For boxing him—was "boxing" the right word exactly, this time?—Tunney received $22,500 . . . and one of the great fight lessons of all time.

Gene had won twenty-nine straight bouts going into this one on May 23, 1922, but he fought Greb with a pair of injured hands and an ailing left elbow. Before the fight a doctor injected adrenalin chloride over his left eye, to prevent it bleeding if an old cut reopened, and shot novocain into the knuckles of both hands.

None of which helped. Greb, smaller, compact, with ailing vision in one eye, was bitter and tough and brawling—and, in every sense of the word, a professional. He knew his trade. In the first ten seconds of the fight, he fractured Tunney's nose in two places and slashed open the cut over Gene's left eye. In the third he cut the other eye. It became a Pier Six brawl dominated by Greb. Tunney, so masterful a boxer before this, simply was outswarmed and outpunched, but he stayed in there.

At the end of the twelfth, dizzy and sick, and with adrenalin trickling into his stomach after Doc Bagley, his second and manager, had made him sniff it to stop nosebleeding, Tunney took a swallow of brandy and orange juice. He came close to being drunk in the ring, and he

47

lasted the full fifteen rounds only by keeping trying.

Before the decision was announced, Gene made his way slowly to Greb's corner. "Harry, you're the winner *tonight*," he said. "Congratulations."

The "tonight" wasn't pure bravado. As early as the third round, with Greb tormenting him, Tunney saw small things here and there—the way Harry dropped his shoulder at times, the move he made when he threw a right hook—and he thought to himself, *I can beat this man.*

And ten months later at Madison Square Garden, he did. He won a split decision in fifteen rounds, a decision he wanted so badly he could taste it. Perhaps it was what his father had said after the first Greb fight. "Why did you let him beat you?" John Tunney had asked. "Twenty-two thousand. It doesn't make any difference whether you received twenty million dollars. You were beaten. You shouldn't let Greb do that."

Gene fought Greb five times in all. Two of the bouts were no-decision affairs, but Tunney kept improving, and after the final bout, in which he beat the old Windmill easily in St. Paul, Greb came into his dressing room after the fight.

"I'm through with you," Harry said. "I'll never fight you again. Let the other guys have a dose of you from now on." After that, Greb became Tunney's greatest fan. Before the Dempsey bout in Philadelphia, he told newsmen he was betting on Gene. Why? "I've boxed them both," he said. "You never know how good Tunney is until you do box him."

HE HAD BEEN fighting as a light-heavyweight; now the strain of getting under the 175-pound limit became too much. He turned his attention fully to the heavyweights, with one exception. On July 24, 1924, Tunney boxed Georges Carpentier at the Polo Grounds in New York, and Carpentier's manager, Marcel Descamps, insisted on Gene coming in under the light-heavyweight limit.

Carpentier already had fought his "match of the century" with Dempsey and had been somewhat discredited, but he still was a game, good boxer with a sharp right hand. Tunney thrashed him, knocking him down four times in the tenth round, but sore hands and near-exhaustion—Tunney resolved never to box at that light a weight again—kept Gene from knocking him out.

Carpentier had been guaranteed $45,000 for the bout —to be taken out of Tunney's take of 55 percent of the gate receipts. The fight drew only $118,000 and Tunney, after paying out the managerial cut (Billy Gibson by now was his manager), sparring partners, training expenses and incidentals, was left with $3000. But he was squarely settled in with the heavyweights.

On June 5, 1925, the hottest June 5 in New York since weather records had been kept—the temperature reached 96—he boxed Tommy Gibbons, who had lost a close decision to Dempsey at Shelby, Montana, in fifteen rounds. This time "boxed" was the specific word. Gibbons was a brilliant dancing master who could hit. He specialized in a double feint climaxed by a left hook to the chin or liver. But Tunney had studied him. When Gibbons went into his routine, Gene simply dropped a short right in on his forehead or left eye and then stepped back. In the twelfth he knocked out Gibbons.

Near the end of June in 1925 Tunney was recovering from a tonsillectomy and touring upstate New York prisons with Bill McCabe, an old AEF friend and the confidential agent to the superintendent of state prisons. At Dannemora, McCabe got a wire from Rickard, asking that he and Tunney come to New York.

A few days later McCabe and Tunney went to the apartment of a friend, Jimmy Eagleton, at Fourteenth Street and Eighth Avenue, and a little later Tex Rickard drove up in his limousine. In the apartment he hung his cane on one arm, took his cigar from his mouth and shook Tunney's hand.

"Gene," he said, "I want to match you to fight Dempsey."

"There's nothing I want more," Gene said.

There was a twinkle in Rickard's eye. "You are going to win the championship from Jack Dempsey," he said. He was kidding.

Tunney wasn't. "All I want is a chance to try," he said.

CHAPTER 4

ON MONDAY, September 27, 1926, summer was
over, suddenly, for New Yorkers; the temperature dropped thirty-five degrees from 86 to 51. The Moderation
League, Inc., which had offices on Madison Avenue, was
in full cry against the demon booze. Drunkenness, particularly among children and motorists, had increased
alarmingly, a League spokesman said, and something
drastic had to be done.

For a day or two, all was quiet on the boxing scene.
Tunney's mother said that Gene had "gone away" and
Billy Gibson said he hadn't seen his charge in more than
twenty-four hours, although over the weekend they both
had been at the Westchester-Biltmore in Harrison. In
Atlantic City, reporters dropped in at Dempsey's suite,

which was heavy with the smell of wintergreen and roses, and Jack, still visibly bruised, said he had nothing to say, no comment about his future, no statement about Tunney.

At the Garden, Rickard broke his big news: an elimination tournament for contending heavyweights, the winner to meet Tunney for the title. Only Harry Wills was barred. Rickard seemed more concerned, however, with a complaint against the federal government. At the Sesquicentennial Stadium, he said, the head Internal Revenue man had demanded a hundred tickets to permit his men to enter and watch the ticket takers at work—after which the agents had run into the arena to watch the bout. Tex said he was going to write to Washington about it.

It was the custom for people to try and sue the new heavyweight champion on whatever grounds could be scraped up—the man had ready money, didn't he?—but the first suit that was an aftermath of the Philadelphia fight was against Dempsey. A man said that Jack, in making his way to the dressing room after the bout, hit his wife in the side with an elbow, causing her to fall. It could have been the best shot Dempsey landed all night.

BY THE MIDDLE of the week, the pot had begun to boil a little again. In Veracruz, Mexico, a hurricane struck viciously with an undetermined loss of life, and the French liner *Paris* steamed into the North River carrying Suzanne Lenglen, the celebrated tennis player, who hiked her skirts for cameramen and said she was in the United States this time to make lots of money as a professional.

52

The World Series was about to start, too, between the New York Yankees with their celebrated "murderers' row" of Ruth, Gehrig, Lazzeri, Meusel and Combs, and the St. Louis Cardinals, but these things were almost apart from the specialized world of fighting. Like horse players, the residents of Cauliflower Row really lived in a world of their own, and that world was prospering.

Billy Gibson had an office in East Forty-second Street. Now, sitting there complacently, he sifted through all kinds of offers for Tunney. The 101 Ranch circus people wanted to put the new champion on display. A theatrical firm offered $100,000 for eighteen weeks of four-a-day time across the country. And so on.

Across the street from the Garden, Dempsey holed up at the Belmont—he and Estelle had come up from Atlantic City for the Series—and played pinochle with Floyd Fitzsimmons, a Midwestern boxing-promoter friend of Jack's.

"I may fight again," he told reporters, "and I may not." He grinned his small-boy grin. "I'm thinking of taking up the practice of law." Kearns's assorted lawsuits still hung over his head. Fitzsimmons nodded and started to tell the newsmen how hard it had been for Dempsey to keep his mind on training before the Philadelphia fight.

"That's enough of that, Floyd," Dempsey cut in. "No alibis. Everything's O.K."

Kearns, who had been tracking Dempsey down in several states legally, now moved to the United States District Court in Manhattan, the gist of his charges being that he had a contract as Dempsey's manager and that Jack owed him hundreds of thousands of dollars in back pay. Dempsey, using the New York lawyers O'Brien,

Malevinsky and Driscoll, countersued and charged that the alleged contract didn't exist.

Not quite all America, meanwhile, had taken Dempsey to its bosom as the lovable Peck's Bad Boy. *Labor,* the trade-union paper, said in an editorial that of the 115,000,000 persons in the United States, 114,000,000 wanted Tunney to win—which, to put it kindly, was something of a distortion of fact. "The American people," the paper said shrilly, "will not forgive a slacker." And: "Nothing in his championship became him like the manner of his leaving it."

There had been no excuses from Dempsey, but there was one from another source. A Dr. Frank H. Russell, with headquarters at the Hotel Astor, said that before the Tunney bout Jack had suffered an infection of the left arm, amounting to an attack of boils. "I am inclined to believe," he said, "that it played a considerable part in the fight. Dempsey was a man intoxicated by poisonous matter in the blood when he entered the ring."

Dempsey, when told, just shook his head. "I lost to a better man," he said again. "I have no alibis."

Tunney, meanwhile, came into town briefly from Connecticut, but somehow missed connections with Gibson. It likely was not deliberate, but there was no mistaking the simple fact Tunney and Gibson were not now the closest of friends. "I'm unacquainted with his schedule," Gibson said tersely when told Tunney had been and gone. Before returning to Connecticut, Tunney invited reporters to accompany him to Philadelphia on the weekend. There was to be, he announced, a reception for boys and girls of the city, and Gene was going there to talk to the boys about how splendid boxing was.

When the World Series started at Yankee Stadium on Sunday, October 3, Dempsey and Estelle were there, taking their seats to tumultuous applause. The scars still were visible on his face. Tunney, meanwhile, had returned from selling boxing to Philadelphia's boys and had gone to West Hartford to stay at the home of his friend Edward S. Dewing and get in a little golf at the Wampanoag Club.

Rickard also turned up at the Stadium, reporting he would have some important announcements to make, but another New York promoter, Humbert Fugazy, stole a march on him. He said he had matched Wills to fight Jack Sharkey on October 12, adding, "I don't see how Gene Tunney can avoid meeting the winner of this fight." He knew very well, of course, how Tunney could and would.

As OCTOBER BEGAN, the country still was busy with its World Series, and even to casual visitors New York seemed an exciting, if crazy, city. In Paris, however, Jacques Deval wrote in *Le Journal* that New York was "a mass of banality, a city of abstinence and desolation, boresome without being noble, a city for which no one could possibly become homesick."

Rickard's important announcement, it appeared, was his plan to build in Manhattan, within the next year, a great outdoor stadium patterned after the Yale Bowl. The success of the Dempsey-Tunney match had been heady and Tex felt that the existing ballparks in New York—the Polo Grounds, the Stadium and Ebbets Field in Brooklyn—no longer were large enough to hold big fight crowds. The new layout, he said, would hold

100,000 football fans and 25,000 more for boxing bouts.

Dempsey returned to Atlantic City with Estelle and Gene Normile, although he was due back in court for the Kearns suit. Tunney held a short conference with Gibson, after which he announced to the press that he had engaged Dudley Field Malone as his attorney and adviser "in all business matters outside the ring." He and Malone, he added, would be going away for two or three days to study contracts and other proposals that had been made.

Meanwhile, Joseph Paul Zukauskas, the Lithuanian who fought under the name Jack Sharkey, came to town with his manager, red-faced, fast-talking Johnny Buckley. Their arrival at the Astor Hotel was, if not exactly a breath of fresh air, at least something different. Sharkey, a onetime sailor with slicked-back blond hair, was a good boxer and hitter, and he was quick-tempered—and cocky. He went up to Stillman's Gymnasium on Eighth Avenue and had a light workout, after which he gathered newsmen around him and told them genially that after he had beaten George Godfrey, the big Negro heavyweight, Godfrey had said Sharkey could beat Wills and Tunney.

That seemed a reasonable statement, Sharkey added.

Both Dempsey and Kearns showed up in court on Tuesday, October 5, but smiled cheerfully at each other. It was, they both knew, merely business. Kearns wanted to get some money out of Dempsey and Dempsey meant for him not to. Jack, on the stand only three or four minutes, charged that Doc had forged his, Dempsey's, name to a contract for one of his bouts and had admitted as much to him at a training camp in Saratoga Springs, New York.

Kearns, meanwhile, introduced into testimony a letter he had written to Dempsey in March, in which he said he had "waited as patiently as possible for you to come to your senses and stop being ungrateful."

"As my vocation is management of boxers," Doc added in the letter, "I have been forced by your actions to assume management of the next heavyweight champion, Napoleon Dorval." Public sentiment, he said, would force a meeting of the two "and he will take the title from you. Put a pin in that and don't say I did not advise you." Dempsey grinned broadly. Life filled with only Napoleon Dorvals for opponents would have been charming.

"These people who are attacking Dempsey," stated Richard L. Mackey, who was defending him, "are nothing but shakedown artists." Decision was reserved for three weeks, for the filing of briefs.

The busy fall days were on. The legitimate theatre season was in full swing on Broadway. At Madison Square Garden, Suzanne Lenglen made her professional debut before 13,000 tennis fans and easily defeated Mary K. Browne. The match was arranged by Charles C. Pyle, who two years before had been an obscure Midwestern promoter. Tex Rickard smiled at the promotion, but kept an eye on Pyle. In St. Louis, Babe Ruth hit three home runs as the Yankees trounced the Cardinals, 19 to 5, and then on Sunday, October 10, the Cards won the title when Grover Cleveland Alexander, tired and hungover, came in from the bull pen with the bases filled and struck out Tony Lazzeri to preserve a 3-to-2 victory. Ruth, it was announced, had broken ten Series records.

But for a moment Chicago was front and center. Gang warfare, sporadic but unending, had spattered the Illinois city ever since Prohibition had been established. Now it seemed to grow more furious. Dion O'Banion, the cut-throat florist, already was dead, and now his successor, Hymie Weiss, was machine-gunned to death on the North Side.

Tunney was in and out of New York, experiencing some of the fringe benefits, if those are the words, of being the heavyweight champion. The New York depart-ment of the American Legion announced it was giving Gene a testimonial dinner on October 28, with 1500 expected. On Saturday, October 9, Tunney went to City Hall, where, looking uncomfortable in a new blue officer's uniform, he was commissioned a first lieutenant in the Marine Reserve Corps, receiving a sword. Pains were taken to note that he wasn't getting the rank be-cause he was the champion. He had applied for a com-mission several months before and it had been granted because of his "distinguished service overseas" with the 11th Marine Regiment.

Five thousand persons filled City Hall Park to get a glimpse of Tunney after the ceremony, which took place inside the Hall in a reception room. They didn't know the officer who was accompanying Tunney. He was Major Anthony J. D. Biddle of the 8th Regiment, Philadelphia. There seemed almost no new social worlds for the cham-pion to conquer.

NEW YORK ONCE again turned its attention to fighting. Forty thousand men, women and children packed Ebbets Field on Tuesday, October 12, to see Sharkey fight Wills, "The Brown Panther." It wasn't much of a bout. The Boston sailor handled the slow-moving Wills with ease, and in the 13th, Wills, after having been warned ten times, was disqualified for backhanding and hitting on the breaks from clinches.

Dempsey, who had returned to town from Atlantic City, moved out of the Belmont and into an apartment on the upper West Side. There was some talk that he might box during the winter at the Tijuana racetrack in Mexico, since Normile, his current manager, was one of the right-hand men of Jim Coffroth, who ran the racecourse. Jack, meanwhile, had nothing to say on boxing, but, rather, turned his attention to horse racing. He had bought four yearlings at the August sales in Saratoga and was anxious to see them run.

There never really was such a thing as Rickard slowing up; he wasn't built that way. But on October 11 he made a slight move in that direction. He went to the Greenbrier in White Sulphur Springs, West Virginia, and took a side trip to Lewisburg, West Virginia, with a twenty-four-year-old, pretty Broadway bit actress, Maxine Hodges, and married her. Maxine, who was to give the free-wheeling promoter a daughter, Maxine Texas, tried hard to get the fifty-five-year-old Tex to ease up and she had some small success at it.

Rickard read of the Dempsey lawsuit with a smile on his face. Kearns had planned that his attorneys would tie up Dempsey's huge paycheck the day after the Philadelphia fight, but he reckoned without Rickard.

The day before the fight Tex went to a Western Union office with a suitcase containing $711,868 in cash for Dempsey. He wired the money to Jack's brother Joe, in California, and there it promptly was placed in a bank vault.

59

"I'll get that hick son of a bitch yet," Doc moaned. "He has crossed me up for the last time."

The rest of October was comparatively quiet along Cauliflower Row. The New York State Athletic Commission, which never had been too fond of Harry Wills, suspended the big Negro for thirty days for his fouling in the Sharkey fight. On October 22 the Garden was filled to capacity, more than 20,000 persons, to see Jim Maloney knock out one Arthur de Kuh in the second round.

It was just an ordinary fight on an ordinary fight night, but there was an intriguing sidelight. Both Dempsey and Tunney were introduced from the ring—and Jack was cheered in an uproar of several minutes, with feet-stamping and paper being showered from the second balcony, while for Gene there were mingled cheers and boos. It bothered Tunney, naturally, but he had become almost used to it by now. He was not the rough-and-ready type that the crowd could identify with, and there wasn't a way on God's earth to make him so.

On October 22, the same night as the Maloney-de Kuh bout, Tunney was saddened to learn of the death in an Atlantic City sanitarium of his old arch-foe, Harry Greb. The great middleweight/light-heavyweight had been in an auto accident several weeks before, and he went into the hospital to have a nose fracture treated. Weak after coming out of the anesthesia, Greb suffered a cerebral hemorrhage and died. The Pittsburgh Windmill was stilled.

Rickard saw Dempsey a couple of times around this time, the idea being to prod Jack into resuming his career, but he had no great luck. After a luncheon with Dempsey on the twenty-sixth, he had to tell newsmen he was doubtful that Jack ever would fight again. "All this talk of my having him under contract to meet Tunney again next year is all bosh," he said. Late in the month Dempsey returned to his home in Los Angeles. Rickard said Jack would resume training there, but no one made any book on it.

Tunney was in Pittsburgh on the twenty-seventh to be a pallbearer at Greb's funeral service. He had come in from Dayton, Ohio, where he already was launched on his round of personal appearances and banquets, and he was to stay in Pittsburgh for several more days to attend the football game between the University of Pittsburgh and Carnegie Tech.

A heavyweight boxing champion at a college football game. There was a feeling that John L. Sullivan was stirring restlessly in his grave.

NOVEMBER CAME, gray and chilly. In London, Sir Oliver Lodge opined that it seemed "absurd to suppose this is the only habitable world," and in Detroit the magician Harry Houdini died of peritonitis after two operations in a week. In Bologna, Italy, a mob killed the boy assailant who fired a shot at Mussolini—the bullet ripped through Il Duce's coat—and the next day hundreds of thousands of Black Shirts paraded in all parts of the country, crying, "Death to every enemy of Mussolini!" In North Dakota, Queen Marie of Rumania, who had come into New York aboard the *Leviathan* on a rainy morning a few days before, had her finger pricked by Chief Red Tomahawk and was given a war bonnet and membership (she was called a "war woman") in the Sioux Nation.

Al Smith was reelected Governor of New York, and the Democrats cut into the Republicans' edge in Congress. *The Ladies' Home Journal,* its latest issue featuring an article on "Sex and Nicotine," offered a year's subscription for a dollar. In Stockholm, Leopold, the heir to the Belgian throne, married Princess Astrid of Sweden in a setting of almost medieval splendor, studded with four kings, two queens and any number of princes and princesses. There was word in London that Asian countries, most notably China, Turkey and Soviet Russia, were forming an "Asiatic League of Nations" as a "hostile counterpoise" to the League of Nations, but here in America there was even more depressing news. Princeton severed athletic relations with Harvard. A Harvard *Lampoon* issue that had needled Princeton with "extreme animosity" had climaxed a long "atmosphere of suspicion and ill will," the Princeton officials charged.

On his way back to California, Dempsey stopped first in Wilmington, Delaware, to visit Estelle's relatives, and then in Chicago, where again he got together with Rickard. Tex was there to confer with Major Frederick McLaughlin, president of the Black Hawks hockey team, about building a stadium like Madison Square Garden for Chicago, possibly the first of a chain of such arenas.

Rickard continued to press Dempsey about the future but with no luck. The big Coloradan continued to brood about losing to Tunney, the fancy Dan. He thought he was through when something like that happened.

Tunney was still being seen in the right places. He went to Bermuda for a holiday of eight days, and when he returned to New York on November 11, he said that he was glad Al Smith had been reelected, since he had contributed to Smith's campaign fund, and that he was ready to begin an eight-week vaudeville tour at $7500 a week.

Coming up the bay toward the North River pier, Tunney stood at attention—it was Armistice Day—when the ship's bugler played taps. Gene told newsmen that eight years before, when the Armistice had been signed, he had received $60 back pay. "It looked like a million dollars to me then," he added.

On Wednesday, November 17, Tunney went to the Hotel Breslin in Manhattan and conferred with Humbert Fugazy.

Fugazy's promotion of the Wills-Sharkey fight had been a financial, if not an artistic, success. He had tasted blood. Now he made his move at muscling in on the big time.

After Humbert had talked with Tunney, Gene emerged and said candidly that he wasn't bound to any one promoter and that Fugazy had as good a chance as anyone for a title fight in 1927. "My services," Tunney noted, "will go to the highest bidder." Fugazy added, "Tunney looked to me straightforward and sincere," and said he felt fairly certain he would land the bout.

Reporters rushed to Rickard. Looking blander than usual, he shrugged and said he had no contract with Tunney. There was a twinkle in his eye, however, as he said he was giving his strictest attention to developing the next challenger for the heavyweight crown.

"And you can bet your last dollar," he said softly, "that when I bring him out, I will have him so tied up he won't be able to move hand or foot." He paused. "Right now, of course, there isn't a single man in the world, with the exception of Dempsey, who could prove an attraction with Tunney."

The split between Tunney and Gibson, meanwhile, seemed to be widening. Billy was with Rickard at the time, and he said almost petulantly that he had no knowledge of Tunney's conference with Fugazy.

BACK HOME in Los Angeles, Dempsey relaxed, looked at his healing face, and plunged into the lighthearted business of having a new home built on Los Felis Boulevard in Los Angeles. Was he going back east? Probably. But first he wanted to go into light training to see "what kind of condition I can get in and what seems to be ahead of me." Did that mean he might or might not fight again? "I won't go into the ring again," he said slowly, "if my condition is in any way objectionable." He gave the newspaper boys a drink and went back to looking at the plans for the new house.

CHAPTER 5

H E W A S B O R N William Harrison Dempsey on June 24, 1895, in Manassa, Colorado, one of the eleven children of Hyrum and Cecilia Smoot Dempsey. When he became a boxer—no, no, a *fighter*—he took the name Jack, after a famous old pug called "Jack Dempsey the Nonpareil." Two of his brothers also used the name, but it stuck to him in the end. In time to come, people were to say he feared no man, but Dempsey never bought that. Nor, indeed, did he buy the whole gilded Dempsey legend. "I wouldn't fight Sam Langford," he said once. "I knew he would flatten me."

From the beginning, fighting was a job to him. Not that he didn't like it. But he had other interests, and when sportswriters started in with their routine about his being a great fighter because he had had to battle to survive poverty, he snorted. "I could have made a life's work out of cowboying or mining," he said. "I was pretty good at both. I dug for everything you can dig for, from coal to gold to uranium."

Dempsey was of Irish and Cherokee blood, chiefly, with a Jewish strain from his father's great-grandmother, Rachel Solomon. At one time Hyrum Dempsey's father was a big politician and landowner in Logan County, West Virginia, and Jack's mother's father owned a good grocery store in Tazewell, Virginia.

Things didn't pan out that well for Jack's parents. Around 1880 Hyrum sold three hundred acres of Logan County coal and timber land at a dollar an acre, and set off in a prairie wagon for Utah with his wife and their two eldest children. They had become Mormons by this time, and they wanted to go west to Mormon territory.

At one time Jack's mother had been given an old book about John L. Sullivan by a magazine seller to whom she had given a glass of milk, and she said before Jack's birth that he would be a boy and would grow up to be a champion boxer like Sullivan.

There were stops, sometimes for a year or more, in places such as Uncompahgre, Montrose, and Steamboat Springs, Colorado; Provo, Utah; and Salt Lake City. Sometimes Hyrum Dempsey was a sharecropper. Sometimes Cecilia Dempsey ran a cheap hash house, such as the Rio Grande in Montrose, an eating place patronized by Denver and Rio Grande workers building the huge Gunnison Tunnel. The children all pitched in, and Dempsey remembered washing dishes at the Rio Grande when he was eleven. "I guess I was a boy for only two years of my life," he said.

There was one time when Hyrum Dempsey made a trip back to West Virginia because he was told—"or told himself," Dempsey said later—that he had 2500 acres of Logan County land due him under his father's will. He found the land had been sold for taxes and he went back to his family, at that time in Provo.

Dempsey, always quick on his feet, found time for athletics in between his dishwashing, shoeshining and newspaper peddling. He ran for the track team and played baseball and basketball in the Provo school, and other times he fished in Lake Utah or hunted and trapped —not for fun, but for food and profit.

He was fifteen in 1910, and his brothers Bernie and Johnny already were beginning to lean toward prizefighting, when Jack put together a homemade punching bag in an old chicken shed behind his house. He painted two faces on it, one white and one black. The white was supposed to be Jim Jeffries, the heavyweight champion. The black was Jack Johnson, the fabulous Negro boxer. When Johnson defeated Jeffries, the young Dempsey rubbed out the white face and painted it, too, black. Awkwardly, savagely, he pounded the bag daily.

A year later he was graduated from school—he hadn't been much of a student, he admitted—and he hit the road.

"I don't think I ever was a bum," Dempsey said later. "I lived in hobo jungles. I begged for work and food; I rode the rods. The difference between a hobo and a bum, I think, is that most bums aren't steady enough to ride the rods—the two-inch narrow steel beams beneath a Pullman. You're only a few inches from the roadbed and if you fall asleep and fall off, you die. I often bet my life that the train would stop and let me off before I shook and shivered my way to my death beneath the wheels."

For years he worked at anything—once he was a porter in the Hotel Utah in Salt Lake City—and he virtually lived in saloons, where he was forever fighting drunks and tough guys. He weighed 130 pounds, and the roughs didn't mind fighting him, he said, "because I sounded like a girl." His high-pitched voice always was the most incongruous thing about Dempsey.

He had his first official fight in Peter Jackson's saloon-gymnasium, run by a man named Hardy Downey, in Salt Lake City. Dempsey got $2.50 for knocking out (in fifteen seconds) a man named One-Punch Hancock, and the same night, for free, he knocked out Hancock's big brother in twenty seconds. He fought every Monday night or so for a while, winning mostly but now and then losing.

All the while, he was learning his chosen business. He even built a low-ceilinged cage, three or four feet high, and practiced sparring in it, so he could perfect the crouch which was to become so famous. He never missed a chance to study fights and fighters. "I learned as a kid," he said, "that no fighter has everything. Hit a fellow on the chin and if he doesn't blink, hit him in the belly. It is as simple as that."

Wherever the freight trains went, Dempsey went. He would con other boxers, like a pool hustler. He rode the rods to Reno and worked out for six or eight rounds in a gym there with a good Negro boxer, Anamas Campbell. He let the other clobber him and Campbell agreed to meet him in a regular bout. Dempsey knocked him out in

68

one round. Said the colored fighter later with a grin, "I knew this white boy was kidding me in the gym. I should never have fought him."

His brothers Bernie and Johnny also went in for the professional game, and Dempsey always thought Bernie would have been a top-notcher—except that he couldn't take a punch on the chin. Once in a while, in some Colorado or Utah town, Johnny and Jack would fight each other for the customers.

By the spring of 1916 Jack was being managed by a Salt Lake City friend named Joe Price, who signed him for a bout at Ely, Nevada, with one Joe Bond of Tacoma, just back from an Australian tour. Dempsey beat him rather easily, but there is a certain small memorableness about the bout for another reason. Bond had just split with his manager, a man named Jack Kearns.

IN JUNE of 1916, sharing an upper berth, Price and Dempsey arrived in hot, humid New York City to see what the pickings were like there. His record in the West had made Jack quite confident—but on the trip to New York, which was a staggered one, taking six weeks, with stops in Kansas City, St. Louis, Chicago and Cleveland, he could only pick up one four-round preliminary bout. No one had heard of him east of the Rockies.

New York wasn't much better. Jack and Price shared a cheap room near the Polo Grounds until they ran out of money. After that, they slept in the parks.

Billy Gibson then was the matchmaker at the Fairmont Club, a good small fight arena, and Price talked Gibson into matching Dempsey with a 215-pound heavyweight named Andre Anderson. Dempsey by this time weighed 162. The fight went ten rounds to no decision, but Jack survived a couple of early knockdowns and was trouncing Anderson at the end.

A boxing writer named Damon Runyon was there, and he thought Dempsey had won. So did Ned Brown of the *World,* who later was to become Jack's good friend and adviser. "He is a great young fighter," Brown wrote. "There is one thing wrong with him, however. He looks like he needs a square meal."

There was a lot of action for Dempsey in New York but not a great deal of money. Joe Price finally hopped a westbound freight early in the fall of 1916, and Jack became the managerial property of "John the Barber" Reisler, a gambler, who promptly matched Dempsey with Langford in Boston. Jack glowered and said nothing doing. "He'd kill me," he said. "I've seen Langford. You're wasting your time. I won't fight him."

Reisler then tried to hook up Jack with Gunboat Smith, another ranking contender, and Dempsey again said no. He wanted to be the top man among fighters, wanted it badly, but he knew what he could and couldn't do at this stage.

Finally, late in 1916, Reisler booked him to fight John Lester Johnson at the Harlem Sporting Club and there was no way out of it. Johnson had fought Langford several times and even had beaten him once. "You dirty no-good louse," Dempsey told Reisler. Then he went in and fought what a couple of writers called a draw with the experienced Johnson—who in the second round broke three of Jack's ribs with a right to the body. "I wasn't beaten," Dempsey said later. "I was massacred."

Disillusioned with the East, Dempsey went back to

Salt Lake City almost immediately. He became a sparring partner for a good heavyweight, Carl Morris, who
paid him seventy-five cents a day and whom Jack learned
to hate. Later Dempsey was to fight Morris three times,
winning all three and knocking out Morris in a minute of
the first round in the last bout. He was, Dempsey said
thoughtfully, "the only fellow that I ever wanted to murder."

ON THIS return to the West, Dempsey married Maxine
Cates of Walla Walla, reportedly a piano player in a
Commercial Street saloon in Salt Lake City. They spent
only a couple of months as man and wife and several
years later were divorced, but Maxine was not completely out of Jack's life.

Three years later, when Dempsey appeared in United
States District Court in San Francisco to answer a charge
of draft evasion, Maxine swore that after their marriage
she had continued to earn a living as she had before
wedding him—by prostitution . . . indicating that Jack
had falsified draft papers in which he had stated he
supported her and other members of his family. The
judge threw out the case and Dempsey was cleared, but
the ugly word "slacker" followed him for years.

JACK KEPT scrambling, changing managers as if they
were dirty shirts. One of them, Fred ("Windy") Windsor, matched him in Murray, Utah, with "Fireman Jim"
Flynn, a "cutie" (who knew all the tricks) of the ring.
Dempsey, whose fingers were still healing from an injury,
was knocked out in two minutes. His brother Bernie,
working as his second, tossed in the towel after four

71

knockdowns. "He'd have killed you with another punch," Bernie said apologetically. It was the only official knockout of Dempsey in his career.

He freighted to San Francisco and then shipped up to Seattle to be a lumberjack, but the call of the wild wasn't that strong. He was back in a Seattle shipyard, catching hot rivets in a tin can, when his mother wired him that Bruce, one of his younger brothers, had been stabbed to death. Dempsey rode the rods back to Salt Lake, but got home three or four hours too late for the funeral. He was still hanging around the Utah city, trying to make his marriage work out—he admitted candidly he was jealous —when out of the blue he got a letter from Doc Kearns. "You still interested in fighting?" Kearns wrote.

It was early 1917.

HE WAS still called Jack Kearns then—Dempsey used to say to him, "You're the doctor," and that was shortened to Doc—and he was a con man through and through. He believed in putting up a big front, and if he had something to sell, so much the better. Jaunty, debonair, he had two items on the credit side: he was a pretty good student of boxing and he knew the business. He often said he had developed Dempsey's left-hand punching by tying his right hand behind him. "Sure he did," Jack would say with a straight face.

Kearns meant business with Dempsey. He had seen him several years before. When Jack wrote back yes, Doc sent him a train ticket and a five-dollar bill and said, Come out to Oakland, California.

That was the beginning of the big ride. Some of the early fights were tough. Dempsey beat Gunboat Smith in

72

a four-rounder in San Francisco—but didn't know about it until he was riding the Oakland ferry later and a second shook him by the shoulders and told him he had won. He met Homer Smith, an All-American type, and knocked him out in Racine, Wisconsin. "I struck a blow against clean living," Dempsey said.

There were the Morris fights. There was Bill Brennan in Milwaukee; Jack knocked him out in the sixth—and heard "Slacker!" from the crowd for the first time. That was February 26, 1918.

Dempsey was becoming known. He fought Fred Fulton, the number-one challenger for Jess Willard's title, in Harrison, New Jersey, for a $12,500 guarantee. Jack wanted to buy a $5000 home for his mother in Salt Lake City. It took Dempsey eighteen seconds to knock out the tall, rangy Fulton, crossing a right over a left. He took the first train to Salt Lake City and bought Cecilia the house.

FOR THE REST of 1918 Jack fought anyone and everyone, mostly second-raters. It wasn't all triumph. He lost a decision in San Francisco to Willie Meehan in a fight that raised $18,000 for the Navy Relief Fund. Then Doc Kearns and Tex Rickard met in Hoboken, New Jersey, and drew up a contract for a title bout with Jess Willard.

The fight was held under a broiling sun in Toledo, Ohio, on July 4, 1919. Willard stood six feet six inches and weighed 250 pounds. Before the weigh-in, Dempsey stuffed himself with bananas and even put rocks into his trunks, and his weight was given out as 188. He was tanned so deeply, Grantland Rice wrote, that he was "burned purple." He was as lean as a man could be; there was no fat, only muscle. He was a picture of compressed energy.

For years after the fight—for tens of years—the story persisted that Kearns had molded plaster of Paris around Dempsey's bandaged hands before the fight, giving him in effect a pair of rocks to throw at Willard. "As God is my judge," Jack said later, "it never happened." It seemed unlikely. Walter Monaghan, a big, burly friend of Willard's, was in Dempsey's dressing room all through the bandaging period.

There may never have been so complete a fighter as Dempsey in the brief bout that followed. Virtually every punch he threw landed. One punch smashed Willard's face and broke his jaw. Dempsey knocked him down four times in the first round and referee Ellie Picard counted the giant out.

"Go on, get outta here!" Kearns yelled at Jack. "Get to the dressing room!" Then, in a couple of seconds, as Dempsey was leaving, Kearns yelled for him to come back. The bell, it seemed, had rung at the count of eight after the fourth knockdown.

It didn't matter, except perhaps to Doc Kearns, who was said to have wagered thousands of dollars at ten to one that Dempsey would knock out Willard in the first round.

Methodically, savagely, Jack beat Jess into submission. Before the fourth round was to start, Willard's seconds threw a towel, the white flag of surrender, into the ring.

Dempsey went to bed, in a Toledo hotel, around 10 p.m. He slept fitfully and had a nightmare in which Willard beat him. He awoke, shakily, got dressed and went down into the street. He stopped a newsboy. "Who won?" Dempsey asked, still dazed. The boy stared at him. "You damn fool," he said, *"you* did." Jack gave him a dollar and went back to bed, the heavyweight champion of the world.

A NEW LIFE of a sort opened for Dempsey. He and Maxine had been divorced before the Fulton fight, and after winning the title he seemed to have turned a corner.

Not that there was an immediate change. He said it himself later: "I was still a bum with a knife and fork, and I dressed like a guy an honest cop would arrest at a carnival."

But, suddenly, drastically, there was more to life than training and fighting. There was Hollywood. Pathé paid Jack $1000 a week to make some action-filled shorts. He was terrible in them but, at that, no worse than most athletes who try to act.

The Big Names of the movies became his friends. Wallace Reid, who was to die of drug addiction, was perhaps closest to him, but Douglas Fairbanks was another good "pal." It was Jack's favorite word for just about everyone. He sparred with Rudolph Valentino— "he couldn't knock your hat off"—and he went dancing with starlets at the Montmartre Café, where, as he put it, he was "a cow on ice." He and Charlie Chaplin were on a first-name basis.

That was part of the time. The rest of it Dempsey spent in New York. There were a thousand and one places to go, speakeasies and legit clubs. Club Richman, Barney Gallant's, the Silver Slipper, Texas Guinan's, Perona's or Jerry Docker's. There was Harlem, too, when

75

things closed up downtown—Connie's Inn, Small's and the Cotton Club. Often Jack, with one party of friends, would run into Doc Kearns with another. They grinned and waved and went their ways.

Rickard became close to Jack and an unofficial adviser. He didn't mind Dempsey going to various clubs, but he warned him about some of the hoods who ran some of them.

"Jack," he said, "those gangster fellers are nice guys, most of them. Be nice to them, polite, but don't never have no business with them. When they own you, they don't let go. And tell that noisy manager of yours the same thing."

Billy Seeman was a man about town at the time and he had a penthouse in Waverly Place in Greenwich Village, where there were parties that Dempsey attended. He met people like Bessie Love and Mabel Normand of the films, Paul Whiteman, Bugs Baer and Rube Goldberg, O. O. McIntyre, Peggy Hopkins Joyce, Bert Lahr and Fred and Adele Astaire.

He was no longer quite such a bum with a knife and fork.

For a few months there was almost no boxing. Then on March 5, 1920, he boxed "three harmless rounds" with an old friend, Terry Keller, in Los Angeles. Later Keller was to end up in a madhouse, as fighters before and after him.

That same month the draft-evasion case came up in San Francisco. It may have been prompted by a celebrated news photograph. A government man had come to Dempsey's hotel in Philadelphia one day and asked Jack to help get men into war work. They drove out to the Sun shipyard and Jack put on overalls and posed for pictures—with patent-leather shoes gleaming in the afternoon sun.

That had started the "slacker" cries, and Dempsey one day decided to join the Navy. The Great Lakes Naval Training Station, where he had done some guest refereeing, had a strong boxing team, including Greb and Pal Moran, and needed a heavyweight. Jack got the necessary enlistment papers, signed them and delegated Doc Kearns to send them in. They never were found.

HE GOT BACK to real boxing on Labor Day in 1920 in Benton Harbor, Michigan, when he fought Billy Miske, an old friend who was dying of Bright's disease and begged Jack to help him get a payday. Floyd Fitzsimmons promoted the fight. Dempsey didn't know whether to "carry" Miske for the whole fight or knock him out quickly. He finally flattened Billy with a right-hand in the third. Kearns and Dempsey split $55,000 and Miske got his payday, $25,000. He didn't live long enough to spend it all.

In December of the same year Dempsey defended his title for the second time, in a rematch with Bill Brennan, who had been doing well since his earlier defeat. Brennan put up a surprisingly strong showing, staggering Jack in both the second and ninth rounds, but Jack left-hooked him to the ribs in the eleventh and knocked him out. Dempsey and Kearns made $100,000 out of that bout, in the old Madison Square Garden, and another $8000 from the movie rights to the fight.

Later Brennan opened a speakeasy and made the mistake one night of throwing out an obnoxious mobster. The hood returned a few nights later and shot him dead.

RICKARD HAD promoted the fight with Brennan, but he had been looking past it. In November of 1920, a month before the Brennan bout, he had signed Dempsey to defend his title against Georges Carpentier.

A good part of the country, whether the charge was true or false, looked on Dempsey as a draft dodger. Carpentier, a handsome Frenchman who never weighed more than 170 pounds, was something else again. He had been four years in the French military service, had been decorated for flying a reconnaissance plane two hundred yards above the German lines and twice had been wounded by shrapnel. He was, all things considered, a genuine War Hero.

The toast of Europe for having defeated a large number of second-raters, Georges first came to New York in the spring of 1920, with a bride and a wardrobe that included seventy-five suits and a hundred silk shirts. Also with him was François Descamps, his manager, who, like Rickard, was looking beyond the farthest horizon. "We will not fight Dempsey," he said pontifically, "until his military affairs are cleared up."

Originally Rickard set up the fight as a co-promoter, his partners being Charles B. Cochran, the famous English theatrical producer, and William A. Brady, his American counterpart. Cochran and Brady ultimately withdrew, however, and Rickard went it alone. He named July 2, 1921, as the date for the bout.

To house the fight, Rickard ordered a 50,000-seat arena built at Boyle's Thirty Acres, a section of New

Jersey's Jersey City. But when the bout "caught fire," he had the stadium enlarged to hold 90,000.

This would be no ordinary fight crowd. Rickard had had a taste of something else and he had liked it. A few months earlier he had promoted a Benny Leonard-Ritchie Mitchell lightweight-championship fight as a benefit for The American Friends of France, the pet charity of Anne Morgan, daughter of one J. P. Morgan and sister of another. Silk hats, dinner jackets and ermine wraps were in the crowd for that fight—the contracts for which, incidentally, were signed in the Madison Avenue home of the Morgans.

That was more like it. Rickard had had "the best people," whoever they were, at one of his promotions and he meant to have them again and again.

He began with the printing of the Carpentier-Dempsey tickets—huge, handsomely engraved cardboards, embossed in gold on the back. And he helped Carpentier decide on his training site—a small estate at Manhasset, Long Island, where the daily spectators included such souls as Vincent Astor and William H. Vanderbilt.

Dempsey, meanwhile, trained at a low-budget hotel in Atlantic City. Well, actually he trained at an abandoned airport nearby, but his headquarters were in the hotel and to it Kearns brought a passel of raffish friends. The first man-sized argument between Kearns and Dempsey took place there after a couple of Doc's chums started a row in a boardwalk café, the Moulin Rouge, and one of them pulled a knife. It was not to be their last argument.

Carpentier was a genial man and a fair enough fighter for a light-heavyweight—he met Dempsey first on a Jersey golf course and said, "Jack, when our fight is done, I hope we will still be such good friends"—but he was, of course, a Frenchman and a businessman, realistic to the core. He went along with the build-up. A hustling publicist-manager, Jack Curley, was recruited to gild the image of the "Orchid Man," and Curley, who at one time had managed the Vatican Choir, British suffragette leader Emmeline Pankhurst and swimmer Annette Kellerman, did a splendid job. He knew fights and fighters, having promoted the disputed Johnson-Willard bout in Havana. The most famous news photograph of this fight seemed to show Jack Johnson being counted out while shading his eyes from the Cuban sun, thus giving rise to his later claim that he had thrown the fight.

Curley stressed the remarkable fact that Carpentier had a "hypnotic eye" and had dispatched several opponents with its magic. He also spoke to the press with awe of Georges' powerful right-hand punching, which on June 23 obligingly knocked out three sparring partners.

Carpentier, through all this, smiled and joked and had a marvelous time. On one particular night he went partying with Edward, Prince of Wales (not yet the Duke of Windsor), and the two of them ended the festive evening by sleeping on the floor in Georges' room.

All the ingredients were there, then, topped by the war-hero-vs.-slacker talk, and even Rickard felt obliged at one point to tell the sportswriters, "For the first time in my life, boys, I am being glutted by free publicity."

It was the first of the grand-scale fights. Rickard hired 1147 employees, including hundreds of ushers, and dozens of special trains went to the fight, including the private cars of Harry A. Sinclair and Edward L. Stettinius. In the working-press rows there were 778 reporters, some from as far away as Tokyo and Copenhagen. The first broadcast of a boxing bout was made by Major J. Andrew White. The spectators included three of Theodore Roosevelt's children, a dozen Biddles from Philadelphia, several Rhinelanders, Henry Ford, Harry Payne Whitney, John D. Rockefeller, Jr., Bernard Baruch's brother Sailing Baruch and a handful of Vanderbilts. Counts and countesses were almost too numerous to mention, and, naturally, show business was there, represented by Sam H. Harris, George M. Cohan, David Belasco and movie star Owen Moore.

The official paid attendance was 77,328, the gate receipts were $1,553,422.15—the first million-dollar gate in the history of boxing. The fight took place in the early afternoon, with the threat of rain hanging over Jersey City. The spectators didn't know of a colloquy between Dempsey and Rickard just before the start.

"Don't kill him, Jack," Tex pleaded in the dressing room. "You'll kill boxing. He's a bum."

Dempsey shrugged. "Tex," he said, "this guy is going out as soon as I can take him. I'm not carrying nobody for nobody, even for you."

Even before the fight began, the big wooden saucer of a stadium had begun swaying, and this was to continue throughout the afternoon. Panic seemed close, but fortunately things never got completely out of hand and the stands lasted the day. Later the builders said the fact that the stadium had swayed *without* falling apart just showed that it had been built well.

The bout lasted three and a half rounds, as the Carpentier myth, nurtured so carefully by Rickard and Jack Curley, came apart at the seams. Once, in the second round, Georges caught Dempsey with a good right-hand and staggered him a little, but after that Jack cut him down ruthlessly. Carpentier finally went down and out, cold, and Dempsey helped carry him to his corner.

THE YEARS tumbled by after that, and generally they were laughers. Dempsey fought some exhibition bouts early in 1922 "for spending money," and in the spring of that year went to Europe for a raffish grand tour with an entourage of Teddy Hayes, clownish Joe Benjamin and the writer Damon Runyon. Nobility fell all over itself to meet the champion, and he in turn charmed them with his directness and simplicity.

Then it was back to work in the States with "tame ones"—one night in Montreal, Dempsey knocked out three men in a single round. Early in the summer of 1923 he boxed Tommy Gibbons at Shelby, Montana . . . of all places. Some Shelby men wanted to put their town on the map and, by scrambling, raised a $200,000 guarantee for Dempsey and Kearns.

It was a grotesque episode. Dempsey set up camp at Great Falls, Montana, seventy miles south of Shelby, and his father was there, along with a cousin, Don Chafin of West Virginia. Jack's training camps, until the later days, always had a laugh a minute and practical jokes went on all day. Dempsey, now twenty-eight, greased his face daily with bear grease and had a cub timber wolf around as a mascot.

It was Indian country, and one day sportswriter Hugh Fullerton asked a Blackfoot, in full war regalia with eagle feathers, whom he liked in the fight. His words, specifically, were: "Who big chief like?"

"Sir," the Blackfoot said, "I happen to like Dempsey.

Gibbons has the skill as a boxer, Dempsey has the power. Power usually prevails over skill." The big chief, it seemed, was a Carlisle graduate.

Dempsey always was savage with his sparmates, and this time was no exception. One of his partners, George Godfrey, the clever Negro, outweighed him by forty pounds, and one day in a workout he cut Jack's face with a right cross. Dempsey promptly left-hooked him and broke two ribs. Earlier, Jack had broken the jaw of Ben Wray, a seven-feet-two-inch cowboy who had sparred with him.

Right up to fight time, there was some doubt that Dempsey and Kearns would get their full cut of the purse—actually, the promoters reneged on $50,000— and the night before the fight, Doc called it off seven times by actual count.

A wooden bowl to accommodate 50,000 persons had been built for the bout. When the fight started, there were some 7000 present—possibly the strangest prizefight audience of all time. There were cowboys, millionaires, Blackfeet, drifters, movie stars and sheep herders; One-Eyed Connolly, the gate crasher; Mrs. Raymond T. Baker (formerly Mrs. Alfred Gwynne Vanderbilt) and Mae Murray, the actress.

Gibbons, at thirty-four, gave Dempsey one of his hardest fights. They went fifteen rounds—like featherweights —and Grantland Rice wrote, "I've never witnessed as much speed in a heavyweight bout." Dempsey won narrowly and handed the lie to the belief that he was purely and simply a slugger. "Don't let anyone tell you Dempsey can't box," the battered Gibbons said. "He knows all the tricks."

Actually, Jack was not in the best of shape for the

fight, a condition he rectified over the rest of the summer, and it was just as well he did. In September he fought Luis Angel Firpo, the "Wild Bull of the Pampas," at the Polo Grounds. It was a night to remember.

Firpo, huge and tousle-haired, had had several fights in the States and had knocked out Jess Willard in six rounds. He seemed almost a club fighter, game and strong, and he knew nothing of the subtleties of boxing.

The Polo Grounds was jam-packed, another of Rickard's successful promotions, and Dempsey was inclined to pooh-pooh Tex's warning: "You watch this guy. He's a good fighter, good right-hand puncher." Jack walked out at the bell, jabbed a few times and then missed a hard right. Firpo cut loose with a wild right on the cheekbone and Jack went down as if pole-axed.

He was out on his feet—but he got up on to them. He went after the Argentinian and knocked him down a half-dozen times, still in the first round. Dempsey was fighting on instinct now. Near the end of the round Firpo half-hit, half-shoved Jack out of the ring and the champion went backward between the top and middle ropes, landing on his neck on Jack Lawrence's typewriter in the front press row.

Helping hands pushed him back, but Dempsey didn't really come to until he was in his corner, sitting on the stool and gasping from the smelling salts Doc Kearns held under his nose. "What round was I knocked out in?" Dempsey asked groggily.

"You just slipped," Doc said. "You're coming out for the second."

Reprieved, Jack went out, more cautiously, in the second, hunting for an opening. When Firpo threw a wild

84

left, Dempsey hit him a right cross and two lefts, all to the chin, and the fight was over.

Dempsey got $500,000 for the Firpo fight—and he got it personally from Rickard, ahead of Kearns, who at this point owed Jack a considerable sum. Doc turned up at Jack's hotel room the next day and smoked at the ears when he saw his charge take out the money Kearns owed him. Then Doc asked Dempsey what he was going to do with all the money.

"I'm putting two hundred thousand in a trust fund," Dempsey said. "At three-four-five percent interest; I dunno."

"You damn fool," Kearns said. "I could get you fifteen percent."

"Doc," Dempsey said, "I'm going to put that money where I know I'll have it when I'm old."

The split between the two had widened.

BY NOW DEMPSEY had made Los Angeles his base. He bought his mother and sister Elsie a $75,000 home at Twenty-fourth Street and Western Avenue and lived with them. But his mother stayed there only a year. She liked the mountain country too much, and Jack then bought her a twenty-two-acre farm outside Salt Lake City and saw to it that his father was living comfortably in Los Angeles.

It was in California, then, that he met and married— in 1925—Estelle Taylor, a beautiful woman whose movie career had been one of ups and downs and now was down. She was witty and warm and had a sense of humor, but she was an actress, with everything that means, and even the easygoing Dempsey didn't have a

85

smooth time living with her. They were married in San Diego before only about fifty friends and relatives—and almost immediately Estelle told Jack that being married to a prize-fighter hurt her socially.

Estelle couldn't abide Kearns, and that was all Dempsey needed to break off definitely with his jaunty, razzmatazz manager. They rented a little home in Hollywood Hills, seeking privacy, and soon they aimed for the moon —a play on Broadway, *The Big Fight,* under the direction of the wispy so-called theatrical genius David Belasco.

"I almost ruined the American theater," said Dempsey later. But Belasco would put on the play and hire Estelle only if Dempsey was in the cast. She got $300 a week and Jack $1000. Dempsey, who played the part of "Tiger," was startled at meeting the ethereal, almost effeminate Belasco, but he was polite and he stuck it out for the run of the play. Six weeks.

There was even a tour in burlesque, with Dempsey's promoters offering $1000 to anyone who stayed three rounds with him. He toured with the Sells-Floto circus at $2500 a week and also played the Palace and Loew's State. He went back to the movies to make some serials, such as *Daredevil Jack* and *Fight and Win,* and even did a full-length film with Estelle, *Manhattan Madness.*

Wanting to get back to fighting, Dempsey became his own manager, guided by Rickard. He went to South Bend, Indiana, and signed with Floyd Fitzsimmons, his old matchmaking friend, to meet Harry Wills. The thought of facing Wills, public opinion to the contrary, never had bothered Dempsey. "These big, slow guys are made for me," he said.

86

Dempsey was supposed to get a million for this fight, the first payment being $300,000 on signing. Instead, Fitzsimmons gave him a handshake and the next day sent him a check for $25,000. "It's all I have," he said, "but there's more where it came from." The next day Dempsey went to the bank, with Fitzsimmons, and discovered there was no money in the account the check had been drawn on. Jack raised general hell and left town.

That was all right with Rickard. He hadn't wanted Dempsey to fight the Negro Wills, perhaps because when Jack Johnson beat Jeffries for the title Rickard had been accused of "humiliating the white race." To add to it, Tex spoke mysteriously of Washington "not wanting the fight."

WITH THE Wills fight shuffled aside, Dempsey had to fight someone, and Rickard picked Tunney.

"Fine," Dempsey said. To him Tunney was just a boxer. Period. He had beaten boxers before.

In the July 1926 issue of *Ring*, the fight magazine, Billy Gibson, Tunney's manager, picked Dempsey as the best heavyweight of all time. "A demon in human form," he was quoted as saying. "The greatest fighter for his weight I have ever witnessed in action." Editorially, the magazine itself was not so complimentary. "Dempsey," it stated in the September issue, "has used the heavyweight title as a medium for almost everything but defense."

Dempsey trained first in California and then at Tom Luther's place in Saratoga, but through it all he never seemed to recapture the feeling he always had had before —the tough, hard, fit feeling. "It was a combination of other things," he was to say later. Kearns had three separate lawsuits after him. He felt logy. Twenty hours before the Philadelphia bout he had dysentery and was given paregoric, the opium solution.

Months after the fight, he told sportswriter Daniel M. Daniel that a week before the bout "I began to realize I was nothing like my old fighting self." He first decided to call off the match or postpone it, then changed his mind. "One day I'd feel good, the next I'd feel rotten," he told Daniel.

When he walked into the ring on September 23, 1926, Dempsey had not fought for three years.

CHAPTER 6

NINETEEN TWENTY-SIX was hurtling toward its close in typical 1920's fashion . . . helter-skelter and nutty. The Prohibition law still was having its strange effect on the life and times of America. Deputy sheriffs in Alabama raided a fishing camp near Magnolia Springs and arrested Governor W. W. Brandon, eight companions and a Negro manservant, whom they found with more than a dozen quarts of "fine old liquor" in their possession. Governor Brandon's previous claim to fame was his stentorian "Twenty-four votes for Underwood!" cry at the 1924 Democratic Presidential convention in New York City.

A strong suggestion was made that poison be inserted into wood alcohol to discourage illegal drinking, but

Secretary of the Treasury Andrew Mellon, who supervised enforcement of the Prohibition law, vetoed it. In Georgia the Ku Klux Klan was riding high, and the country's divorce rate was rising swiftly. The stock market still was everyone's baby and the Broadway theater was prospering mightily; there were seventy or so plays and musicals to choose from. The main stem's most unusual attraction was *The Ladder,* a play about reincarnation, to which admission was free, courtesy of Edgar B. Davis, a Texas millionaire who believed fervently in the theme.

Abie's Irish Rose was in the fifth year of its run. There was momentarily no *Ziegfeld Follies* on Broadway, but Flo's heirs apparent, George White and Earl Carroll, had their respective *Scandals* and *Vanities* on display. The movies still were silent but were on the verge of becoming "talkies," and some of the big names enjoying their last year or two as stars were Pola Negri, Lya de Putti, Francis X. Bushman and the tragic John Gilbert, the screen's great lover who, it turned out, had a voice even higher and squeakier than Dempsey's.

Advertising was really beginning to take a hold on the public, and the people knew all the slogans. They knew "Even Your Best Friend Won't Tell You" meant Listerine, and "It Floats" was, of course, Ivory Soap. The Hogarth of the day was John Held, Jr., whose drawings of the flapper, all planes and angles, were featured in *Life.*

On Sunday, November 21, the Irish Free State announced it had insisted that the term "United Kingdom" be eliminated from the official name of the British Empire, that the Dominions have absolute equality, that the

King's title be changed to match the changed status of the Irish Free State and that each state be free to conduct its own affairs and sign treaties.

Nobody paid much attention.

IN NEW YORK, Teddy Hayes, Dempsey's old confidant and "secretary," filed a $60,000 suit against the former champion, and Jack said he would return within two months to defend himself in the court action. Rickard, meanwhile, was mulling over a new scheme: an elimination series of bouts by the leading heavyweights to produce a contender for Tunney. "Perhaps Sharkey," he mused, "and Harry Persson, Monte Munn and Paul Berlenbach." Berlenbach, the "Astoria Assassin," was the former light-heavyweight champion. "And," Tex added, "Dempsey, I should think."

In California, Dempsey had no comment. It seemed obvious he had no idea whether he would fight again.

Fugazy loomed larger as a competitor for Rickard. He already had contracted for Ebbets Field, the Brooklyn Dodgers' ballyard; now he got the rights for the summer of 1927 to the Polo Grounds, the Giants' stadium. Rickard's only announcement along these lines was to say that he didn't know whether Tunney would work for him but he hoped to know shortly. He didn't seem terribly worried.

Tunney, meanwhile, had begun his vaudeville tour, and when he came into New York City late Sunday night, November 28, to start an engagement at Loew's State Theatre, he took the occasion to deny once again that he and Gibson were on the outs—although it seemed apparent to most people that they were. "Gibson and myself," Gene said, "are going along just as we always did. The idea that I intend to pull away from him is ridiculous."

Tunney had no comment on what had caused the change in his attitude toward Rickard and working for him. Right after the Dempsey fight, he had said publicly that Tex would promote his first title defense.

ON WEDNESDAY, December 2, the *Baltimore News* came out with a story that seemed in no way to be linked with, or to have been prompted by, Tex Rickard—and yet if the old ballyhoo master had wanted to pep up interest in a return Dempsey-Tunney match, he couldn't have started off his campaign in better fashion.

The head of the security force at Dempsey's training camp before the Tunney fight had been Police Captain Charles J. Mabbutt of Atlantic City. Now, in a signed article in the Baltimore paper, Captain Mabbutt came out flatly and said that poison had been put into Dempsey's coffee on the Saturday morning before the fight.

According to the Captain, he, Dempsey and Jerry the Greek, Jack's faithful trainer and man of all work, each felt that "a poisonous substance was introduced into the cream used by our party" at breakfast. Captain Mabbutt said the three of them, together with Sergeant Mike Trent, a Chicago detective hired as Dempsey's bodyguard, had breakfast "as usual" at the Carney Cottage in Atlantic City about 7:00 a.m. that Saturday. Trent, the Captain added, had taken his coffee black, but the others used cream and, according to the Captain, all suffered.

After that Saturday, Dempsey did no training except for a little bag punching before breaking camp. "He was an ill man," Captain Mabbutt declared.

The reaction elsewhere was quick—and negative.

In Chicago, Sergeant Trent said the whole story sounded hokey to him. For one thing, he declared, he always took cream in his coffee. "Furthermore," he added, "I don't remember seeing Mabbutt at any meals with the Dempsey party. He ate in another part of town."

Trent said it was his opinion that Dempsey was not himself in the Philadelphia fight, "but he was not poisoned. Or if he was, it was done in some mysterious way after the fourth round."

"Philadelphia Jack" O'Brien, the famous former boxer who had been Dempsey's chief second at the fight, said "the only poison Jack got was that first-round punch of Tunney's to the jaw." O'Brien said that three minutes before the fight, he would have bet five thousand dollars to a thousand on Dempsey "but not one nickel, three minutes after it started." He also stated that he didn't recall Captain Mabbutt being around Dempsey during the last few days before the bout.

Gibson, in Cleveland with Ray Campbell, one of Tunney's personal representatives, scoffed at the charge. Back in New York City, Rickard said blandly, "Put it down as a lot of bunk. Dempsey told me, as well as others, that it was the bunk."

If Dempsey had wanted an alibi for his poor showing, Captain Mabbutt had provided one. But the next day in Los Angeles the former champion denied the whole story. "I probably had a touch of ptomaine a week or so before the fight," he said, "but that hadn't anything to do with the result." And in New York the famed roughneck cop Johnny Broderick, who had been another of Dempsey's bodyguards, said there was nothing to the report. Broderick said he, Detective Jack Smith, Jerry the Greek and Dempsey were the ones at the breakfast table that morning.

Tunney, during all this, was playing the four-a-day time at Loew's State, where *The Temptress* was on screen, and he smiled as he read the reports. They probably were, as Rickard had noted, bunk, but if one was to be cynical, of course they didn't hurt the build-up for a return bout.

IN PARIS, movie audiences went wild over *The Big Parade,* while in Beverly Hills, Lita Grey Chaplin had "fled" with her two children to her grandfather's home, according to her lawyer, and said, "I'm never going back . . . never, never, never!" when reporters asked her about her broken marriage to Charles Chaplin. Her attorney, George Beebe, said thoughtfully he didn't know if he would ask for one million dollars or two, in the property settlement. Winter had come early over America, and in New York the mercury went to twelve above zero. More than a hundred Great Lakes steamers were caught in ice jams, temporarily stranding two thousand seamen, and in Great Britain, George Bernard Shaw said vehemently it was his belief that smokers should be prosecuted and the manufacture and sale of tobacco prohibited.

IN NEW YORK the twin promoters, Rickard and Fugazy, continued their paper battle. Rickard said he had Jack Sharkey signed to agreements to face Berlenbach, Persson and Jim Maloney. "If he survives these three," Tex said, "he may meet Dempsey." Fugazy said he had a prior contract with Sharkey matching him with Jack Delaney, and planned to hold him to it.

Rickard added that he had received a telegram from Dempsey saying Jack would be in New York City shortly after January 1, 1927. Tex hinted that Jack had reversed his field and had decided to box again and that he wanted a return match with Tunney. "It is perfectly natural for Dempsey, having decided to return to the ring as I knew he would, to want to fight Tunney," Rickard said with a straight face.

Tunney's days continued to be busy. On Thursday, December 9, he was named an honorary deputy county clerk of King's County in New York, and a gold badge was pinned onto him by a woman court clerk. Gene, in a brief speech, said he would like to be a model to the youth of America.

The fight game went on. On December 16, Sharkey kept busy by knocking out Homer Smith in Syracuse, afterward calling off his December 20 fight with one Sully Montgomery, saying he had injured his right hand in flattening Smith. At the Fourth Regiment Armory in Jersey City, Delaney knocked out heavyweight Bud Gorman. The evening was most notable for the fact that the first bout of the night ended in a draw between a fighter named Doc Conrad of Elizabeth, New Jersey, and James J. Braddock, a Union City light-heavyweight. Braddock, a Jersey longshoreman, was just starting the long career that would lead him to the heavyweight title in the Thirties and his nickname, "The Cinderella Man."

A couple of Rickard's heavyweight-tourney eligibles fell by the wayside. Jim Maloney, the Bostonian, took

95

care of one by decisively defeating Harry Persson, the European champion, before 15,000 fans at the Garden. Knut Hansen gave Monte Munn a bad beating in another fight.

Jess McMahon, Rickard's Garden matchmaker, promptly signed Maloney to three winter fights, against Delaney, Sharkey and Hansen, with "possibly" a fourth bout against Dempsey. Meanwhile, Rickard had bought up 30,000 common shares of Madison Square Garden stock at fifteen cents a share. Vice-president and Treasurer William F. Carey of the Garden denied that a disagreement between Tex and John Ringling had motivated Rickard's speculation.

In Los Angeles, Dempsey indicated for the first time that he was thinking seriously about coming back. Twelve pounds over his fighting weight, he put on a gymnasium suit and worked out briefly but briskly. He said that if he did fight again, he'd like to meet Tunney in New York either on May 30 or July 4, preferably at the earlier time.

The Kearns litigation was dragging on. It had been determined by this time that his claims totaled $519,000.98, and a New York court granted permission to remove the case to the jurisdiction of a United States District Court in Philadelphia.

THE COUNTRY was prospering as never before. United States Steel announced that its 86,000 shareholders had received $203,321,000, or a forty-percent dividend, the highest in history. At the Vatican, Pope Pius XI condemned fascism but praised Benito Mussolini as "the man who with such energy governs the fate of Italy." On

Saturday, Christmas Day, Japan's Emperor Yoshihito, forty-two, died of pneumonia and was succeeded by the Prince Regent, Hirohito, who for five years had been directing his country's destiny while Yoshihito was ailing. Born in 1901, Hirohito became the 123rd emperor of Japan in a line "unbroken for all eternity." In his first message as emperor, he committed Japan to peace.

On Sunday, December 26, *The New York Times* came out with a front-page story to the effect that the world had almost lost its new heavyweight champion.

At Rockwood, Maine, Tunney, his host Pert Fowler and two other men were crossing frozen Moosehead Lake—where in spots the water is more than a hundred feet deep—en route to Christmas-morning Mass. In trying to leap an ice wrinkle Tunney lost his footing, the *Times* stated, plunged into the water, and was only saved, at a point halfway across the lake, by a human chain of the other men with him.

"That was the closest call I ever had," Tunney was reported saying in the Rockwood Hotel, where he stayed in bed until his clothes dried. "I'll never forget this Christmas." The party of men then returned to their camp at Tomhegan Point, traveling ten miles by automobile and walking the last four miles rather than try the lake again.

Tunney's later version was a bit different. He had gotten soaking wet, he said, but only from the water around the broken ice. "I was never really in danger," he said. It didn't matter. It made a good story.

As the year drew to a close, boxing experts took a glance at the almost incredible popularity of the sport in the country. Dawson of the *Times,* in his year's review, took an amazed look at the astronomical purses Dempsey and Tunney had received at Philadelphia, and compared them with the $27,500 that Dempsey had earned in his fight with Willard at Maumee Bay in Toledo. Tex Rickard gave out some Madison Square Garden figures that were pretty staggering. In 1924, 1925 and 1926, he said, the Garden had grossed $7,790,993.13, paying $389,549.65 in state taxes and $779,099.31 in federal taxes during that time. Boxing, of course, brought in most of the revenue.

It wasn't only boxing. Leading American bankers and businessmen, queried as 1926 came to its end, said they had "conservative optimism" about 1927.

Fugazy kept busy, trying to buck Rickard. He said he was trying to match Delaney with Tunney for a summer bout at the Polo Grounds, but in Lewiston, Maine, Gene denied he had any such plan. Fugazy said 98,000 persons could be shoehorned into the Polo Grounds—"Dempsey and Firpo grossed $1,228,000 there"—and on Thursday, December 30, he had a talk with Tunney about it. Gene merely said that Fugazy had made a "very liberal offer" but that he would await any and all other proposals.

Gibson, incidentally, sat in an anteroom with newsmen during the discussion and did not take part in it. In a statement to the reporters, Tunney said he didn't care who he fought "just so long as it is a man who will draw the most money or who is the biggest card."

With that, he took the 6:05 p.m. train for St. Louis to continue his vaudeville tour. He would be back east, he said, in March.

* * *

ALABAMA TIED Stanford in the Rose Bowl football game on New Year's Day, and those Americans who were not too hung-over to listen to the radio heard the game broadcast, over an unheard-of national hook-up of nineteen stations, by Graham McNamee.

Mr. McNamee was something else again as an announcer. Not always accurate and frequently given to wandering from the topic at hand—"Ah, the sun shining on those California hills is a wonderful sight, I tell you!" —he was the best-known sports announcer of the day. Possibly because his broadcasts generally seemed tinged with hysteria. America wasn't exactly on the verge of a nervous breakdown, but its pace had quickened so and its search for fun was so headlong, that just a smidgeon of hysteria seemed appropriate for a radio performer.

President Calvin Coolidge spent the day quietly and with customary silence in the White House. Someone of the time said that "whenever Coolidge opens his mouth to speak, a moth flies out," and it wasn't too facetious at that.

Weatherwise, it was a normal New Year's. New York City had gotten through a rainy Eve and only a comparative handful had been taken ill from bootleg liquor, which included that year such holiday specials as fake champagne (carbonated cider and grain alcohol) at $100 a bottle. Marines were sent to Nicaragua to protect American property. Some financiers worried that the soldiers' bonus from World War I, due to be paid in two days, would harm the nation's economy.

Hollywood prepared for another big year. There were bright young newcomers on hand—Gary Cooper, Gilbert Roland and Nancy Carroll, for instance—and the estab-

99

lished stars such as Thomas Meighan, Lon Chaney and Wallace Beery. Gloria Swanson had just come back from Europe with a new name, having wed the Marquis Henri de la Falaise de la Coudraye. Clara Bow was making from $3000 to $4000 a week. A big-eyed, dark-haired girl fresh from dancing in a New York café, Miss Lucille Le Sueur, had changed her name to Joan Crawford and was on her way up.

Lee Tracy was the star of *Broadway,* the big legitimate theater hit of which Alexander Woollcott had said it "perfectly caught the accent of the city's voice." Gertrude Lawrence was appearing at the Winter Garden with Victor Moore in *Oh, Kay!,* Beatrice Lillie was in *Oh, Please!* and Ethel Barrymore played in Maugham's *The Constant Wife.* There were some seventy-five plays and musicals on the main stem. It was about par for the course in the Twenties.

There was an announcement from Walter S. Gifford, president of the American Telephone and Telegraph Company. Early in January, he said, a wireless telephone service would be opened between New York and London, costing $75 for three minutes' conversation and $25 for each extra minute.

It was a remarkable world, so full of a number of things.

THE BOXING BEAT was comparatively quiet in the first few days of 1927.

The only noteworthy news was the apparent widening of the breach between Tunney and Billy Gibson. Gibson had a conference with Tex Rickard at Madison Square Garden, but no one knew whether it dealt with Tunney's affairs or with those of the lighter fighter, Lewis "Kid" Kaplan, whom Billy also managed. Tunney, branching into the Midwest with his vaudeville tour, arranged to meet with Rickard, Gibson, Dudley Field Malone and others in St. Louis. From there, Dawson of the *Times* said there had been a threatened break in Gibson-Tunney relations, with Rickard acting as peacemaker behind "locked or guarded doors."

Apparently the two men had argued about whether Tunney should turn over a percentage of his earnings to Malone, his new legal adviser, but when the stormy session ended, Gene told sportswriters all was serene. "No contract up to tonight has existed between Billy and me since last February," he noted, but in a day or so new contracts would be drawn up and "then Billy will be in the same position as before."

Before going to St. Louis, Rickard had conferred with Jack Delaney at the Hotel Astor, but Fugazy, still scrambling to get a piece of the action, said he had offered Tunney a $585,000 guarantee to box Delaney.

The big news came out of St. Louis on Thursday, January 6. Rickard announced that he had signed the heavyweight champion to defend his title some time after July 1, the date and place to be announced forty-five days before the match.

Tunney had been guaranteed just what Dempsey had gotten for the Philadelphia fight—a flat $475,000 and 50 percent of the gate-receipts net over one million dollars. Rickard tried to get Gene to sign a post-fight option, but this was rejected by the boxer.

"In signing to box for Mr. Rickard," Tunney announced to the reporters, "I tinged business with a little sentiment, or loyalty, if you will." Even if Tex's offer had been matched, he added, he "would have stayed with the man who gave me the chance at the title." Then he wired Fugazy in New York: "Regret we could not get together. Warmest regards."

Rickard, his day's work well done, gathered his entourage and took the 4:00 p.m. train back to New York.

CHAPTER 7

As 1927 started, George Lewis Rickard was fifty-six. He had only two more years to live.

Rickard was by far the most celebrated promoter of his time, and his name was synonymous with larger-than-life sporting events. He had, however, lived a half-dozen previous lives, and the public at large wasn't aware that he had been a cowhand, a Texas marshal, a prospector for gold in Alaska, a successful gambling-joint-and-saloon owner in the Klondike and in Nevada, and a large-scale rancher in Paraguay. The truth was, he never had lived in a city, a real city, until he was forty.

He seemed a contradiction of a man. He could be cunning, shrewd and almost ruthless in his manipulations, but he also had a seemingly deserved reputation for directness and honesty. And apparently he was gullible. For a brief period Gene Fowler was his press agent, and Fowler never ceased wondering at the abandon with which Tex plunged into buying phony stock, putting money into worthless land and backing foolish inventions.

One had one's pick of birthplaces for Rickard. He would say at times that it had been Kansas City, Missouri; then he would change it to Kansas City, Kansas. Once he said it had been Wyandotte, Kansas, and then there was his mother's version, which was that he had been born in Clay County, Missouri. In either 1870 or 1871.

He did grow up in the Clay County area, however—a bloody strip of land along the Kansas border, where Jesse and Frank James and the Youngers prowled, and where Quantrill's infamous Black Flag Brigade appeared now and then. It was so turbulent a community that the Rickards moved to Cambridge, Texas, where Tex earned his first money shining cowboys' boots on the town's lone street.

By eleven or twelve, Dink, as he was called, became first a horse wrangler and then, a little later, a trail driver. Later he never thought it unusual that he had done such work at such a tender age. "I was a little man just as the others were big men," he said, "and both of us had our work to do."

After a few years as a cowboy, Rickard in 1894 was elected city marshal of Henrietta, Texas. He also married Leona Bittick, daughter of a physician. They had a baby boy, but both Leona and the infant died early in 1895.

Rickard lost interest in Henrietta, his job as marshal

and just about everything else. To the north, the great Alaska gold rush had begun. Later in the year he headed for the action. For the rest of his life, Tex never was to be too far removed from where it was.

BOOKS HAVE been written about the Alaska gold rush, and poems and songs written, but no one really has been able to say exactly how it was. There was a character or a celebrity around each corner. Wyatt Earp and Lucky Baldwin were there and, some say, Calamity Jane. Jack London and Rex Beach were on hand and so was Wilson Mizner, the gambler-hustler-wit. The citizens included Alexander Pantages and Sid Grauman, who were to make it big as movie and vaudeville impresarios, and Key Pittman, who was to become a United States Senator from Nevada. Marjorie Rambeau, then a child singer and actress but later to become the toast of Broadway, sang and played the banjo for a time at Rickard's Northern Saloon in Nome.

Tex started out as a gambler and barkeep. His early idol was Sam Bonnifield, best known of the gambling men in the Yukon, and he had his first shot at being an employer when Bonnifield, on starting a fancy gaming house, gave Rickard the old shack he had been using, complete with craps and roulette layouts, chips, cards and liquor.

Rickard ran it, but he also gambled on the side—and in two weeks lost the whole thing.

He drifted through the Yukon. For one fifteen-month stretch he worked in Dawson as a $20-a-day bartender and faro dealer. Then he managed to open his Northern Saloon in Nome late in the 1890's. It was an almost instantaneous success. The bar receipts on opening day alone were $935, and in four years Rickard cleared almost half a million dollars. But Tex liked to gamble. He had little of the money left when finally he returned to the United States.

It was a remarkable gold strike, over all, of course. In the first two years of the Alaskan rush, $7,500,000 in gold was produced, and in the first decade the total was $118,725,000.

STILL AS RESTLESS as ever, Tex went to South Africa to hunt diamonds. He didn't find any, but he did find Walter Fields, a vaudeville comic, and his brother, W. C. The Fieldses, who were on an around-the-world tour, rolled into Cape Town in a wagon that had been converted into a horseless carriage but from which the engine had fallen. It was W. C., Rickard said later, who turned to Walter and said grandiosely, "Walk back and get it. You'll find me in the nearest saloon with this gentleman"—he indicated Rickard—"here."

Tex became their number-one fan, in Cape Town, and always insisted that Walter was funnier than W. C.

On February 15, 1905, Rickard and two partners, Kid Highley and Jim Morrison, opened another Northern, this one in Goldfield, in southwestern Nevada, where another gold rush was in progress. And it was there in Goldfield that he got into the business for which he was to become famous—boxing. On Labor Day, September 2, 1906, he promoted a lightweight championship bout between Joe Gans, the Negro boxing master from Baltimore, and Battling Nelson, a crude, foul, hard-as-rock fighter called the "Durable Dane."

Rickard paid $50 per thousand feet for 214,667 feet of green lumber and, in a desert a half-mile from Gold-field, he had built a big wooden saucer that would hold 7926 persons. The fans who jammed into the arena paid $69,715, and Tex ended up clearing $13,215 for himself.

The fight itself long has been considered a classic. The great Gans, considered by some to be the most remarkable boxer of all time, put up with Nelson's butting and kicking for forty-two rounds and, meanwhile, gave the other man a tremendous boxing lesson. In the forty-second, Nelson hit low so deliberately that he was declared the loser on a foul.

Rickard's appetite had been whetted. Early in 1910, Jack Johnson, the controversial Negro heavyweight champion, and former champion Jim Jeffries, who had been in retirement, signed a pact to fight in July of that year. Then they asked the leading sports promoters of the world to bid for the right to promote the fight.

Tex figured that Jeffries already had been signed up by one of the promoters, so he concentrated on the gay, arrogant, witty Johnson, of whom Damon Runyon once wrote: "I always thought that John Arthur at his best would have been too much for Jack Dempsey. He would have smothered up the rushes of the Manassa Mauler, it seems to me, and gradually cuffed him into submission."

Rickard stuffed a bag with thousand-dollar bills and went to Pittsburgh, where Johnson was performing in vaudeville. He first saw Johnson's white wife (who later was to kill herself).

"I'd buy you just about any kind of present you'd like,

Mrs. Johnson, if you could talk him into signing up with me," Rickard said.

"A fur coat?"

"You got yourself a deal, ma'am."

Then Tex went to see Johnson, who candidly admitted his high living had left him broke. Rickard put $2500 in new bills on his dressing table. "Jack," he said, "if you agree to fight for me, I'll see that no one takes advantage of you."

Johnson—"L'il Artha"—smiled and showed his mouth full of gold teeth. "Yes, sir!" he said. "And I'll tell you something else you should know. They're gonna bid $100,000 for this fight. If you put in a bid for $101,000, you'll get it sure."

Rickard then went to New York and talked with Jack Gleason, a onetime actor and playwright, who had Jeffries in his pocket. Rickard closed a deal to promote the fight in partnership with Gleason, if their bid was successful. It was—and the fight was scheduled for San Francisco. In 1910, reformers had succeeded in getting boxing banned in all the West except California and Nevada.

Governor James N. Gillett, however, suddenly banned the fight in California, too, and it was shifted to Reno, Nevada.

Fifteen thousand saw the bout, in the hot Western sunshine, and despite the rather childish machinations of James J. Corbett, the former champion—who stood near a neutral corner and made faces at Johnson and sarcastic remarks, which Johnson topped easily with much wittier comments—the Negro knocked out the onetime boilermaker in the fifteenth round, when Rickard, who refereed the fight himself, stopped it. A sportswriter named Portus Baxter sent this lead to his paper, the Seattle *Post-Intelligencer:* "The black wins!"

THE FIGHT AND its aftermath must have left their mark on Rickard. In the North, especially, a number of race riots broke out, and eleven persons were killed in them. Congress was so upset by the national reaction to the bout that it passed legislation banning the interstate transmission of fight films which remained federal law for the next thirty-eight years. Public showings of motion pictures of this fight were considered by Congress to have helped trigger the riots.

This could have been the actual cause of Rickard's later barring Harry Wills as an opponent for Dempsey. Jeffries, however, had no alibis. "I could never have whipped Jack Johnson at my best," he said.

Near the end of 1910, Tex took time out from promoting to become, of all things, a cattle rancher in South America. With $400,000 to invest, he bought 325,000 acres of land in the Gran Chaco in Paraguay, as well as 50,000 cattle.

In South America, where he lived stylishly with a glittering $10,000 British limousine among his assets, Rickard met former President Theodore Roosevelt on the yacht-gunboat of the President of Paraguay. Roosevelt was impressed by Rickard, and remained one of his admirers always.

After four and a half years of South America life, Rickard returned to New York early in 1915 with his second wife, Edith Mae. There he met for the first time Jess Willard, the tall and brawny Kansan who had beaten

Johnson for the heavyweight title in Havana just a short while before.

Intrigued by Willard's size and potential as a giant who had to be slain, Rickard plunged back into the promoting business. He rented Madison Square Garden for $15,000 and staged a match there between the big champion and a red-haired sailor named Frank Moran, whose only asset was a right-hand swing that sportswriters called "Mary Ann." They met on March 25, 1916—with socialites mingling with the regular fight crowd, and even a couple of hundred women on hand —and Willard won handily. Rickard reported that the gate had been $152,000, largest in history for an indoor attraction, and he netted $42,000 for himself. "I'm satisfied that the fight was a success," he said, "that the public has no kick, and you newspaper fellows can't say anything terrible about me."

The next year, after unrelenting pressure from William Randolph Hearst in his *New York Journal,* the State of New York barred boxing.

Around this time the young Dempsey was beginning to make himself known, and one night Doc Kearns, his manager, met Rickard at the Biltmore bar in New York, where Kearns was drinking with John McGraw, the Giants' manager.

"What about my boy fighting Willard?" Kearns asked casually.

"The champ's too big for that little feller of yours, Doc," Rickard said.

But Dempsey kept fighting and kept knocking out opponents, including the skillful Fred Fulton in 18.6 seconds, and Rickard began to look his way. There was one day, for instance, when he dropped in on Dempsey and Kearns at their room in the Hotel Claridge in New York. He looked at Dempsey and shook his head. "Every time I see you," he said, "you look smaller to me."

The duel of words between Kearns and Rickard was a masterly colloquy between two con men, but finally Rickard signed Dempsey, for a fee of $27,500, to fight the giant Willard. Then Tex had an 80,000-seat stadium built, at a cost of $100,000, near Maumee Bay, outside of Toledo.

Financially, the fight, on July 4, 1919, was a bust. Less than 20,000 persons attended, and the gross receipts were only $452,522; after expenses, Rickard ended up with a small loss. In other ways, however, it was a success. It was presented as a gaudy show, with, among other attractions, an Army aviator climbing from an airplane in the sky and going up a rope ladder to another plane flying above it. Again the socialites turned up, including Major Biddle, who brought a detachment of Marines into the ring for an exhibition of bayonet and dagger fighting. He and Rickard were the judges, and Warren Barbour, who was to become a United States Senator from New Jersey, was timekeeper.

It was just before this bout that Rickard gave Dempsey the first of his little pre-fight talks. "If he hits you hard and hurts you a lot and you think he is going to kill you," Tex said, "you just go down and stay down. Don't think about me. It will be all right with me. I don't want you to get killed."

He didn't have to worry. In one of the great prizefighting exhibitions of all time, Dempsey beat Willard into total submission. Willard's seconds threw in the towel before the fourth. A twenty-three-year-old Chicago reporter named Charles MacArthur helped Willard out of the ring and down the aisle to his dressing room. As he stumbled along, the bleeding Willard mumbled, "I have $100,000 and a farm in Kansas. I have $100,000 and a farm in Kansas. . . ."

ARMED WITH an authentic, colorful product to merchandise in Dempsey, Rickard set about creating his early masterpiece: the Dempsey-Carpentier fight of July 2, 1921.

Paul Gallico, the New York sportswriter, theorized that Rickard became successful as a promoter by presenting fights in which one boxer was considered a hero, the other a villain.

Dempsey, already hounded by the cries of "slacker," was a ready-made villain; Carpentier was a natural white knight in shining armor. The Dempsey draft-evasion charges already had been dismissed by a federal grand jury in San Francisco, but the taint lingered.

Rickard toyed around with several plans involving the wages to go to the fighters. He finally paid Dempsey and Carpentier $500,000 each. With gate receipts in excess of $1,500,000, Tex admitted modestly he had made $400,000 or so for himself.

He was proudest, however, of the caliber of the crowd, with its Roosevelts, Vanderbilts, Goulds, Astors, Baruchs and Rockefellers. "Look at all them fine people," Tex kept saying as the crowd swelled. He even escorted one guest personally to a better seat when the guest—John D. Rockefeller, Jr.—complained he couldn't see too well.

Rickard got a tremendous amount of free publicity in the newspapers for the bout, of course—and, according to Jack Kofoed, a sports columnist for the New York *Evening Post,* some that was not quite so free. "Rickard," Kofoed wrote, "called in the boxing writers who had taken money in the past and told them what he wanted." The columnist said Tex gave $500 to this one, $1000 to another—a procedure he apparently kept up until, in 1927, pressure from New York publishers forced him to spend $15,000 advertising the Dempsey-Sharkey fight.

The fight, of course, was something of a joke. Carpentier fell apart after the first good punch Dempsey landed.

No ONE ever had claimed that Rickard was a saint, but generally his character was considered excellent, at least for a fight promoter.

It had to be when in January 1922 two adolescent girls, who had run into Bellevue Hospital with clothes torn and tears on their faces, accused him of having tried to attack them in daylight in a taxicab. Tex was arrested on charges of having had immoral relations with underage girls.

Under questioning, the girls said they had been intimate with Rickard the previous summer, after having met him at the Garden swimming pool.

Rickard's friends, influential, social and wealthy, came quickly to his defense. Major Biddle, for instance, called him "the finest and noblest sportsman I ever knew. He is strait-laced in every respect, and the soul of honor."

His trial began on March 20, 1921, with Chief Assistant District Attorney Ferdinand A. Pecora prosecuting and the brilliant Max D. Steuer defending Rickard. The witnesses included Kermit Roosevelt, who lauded Tex and said that he didn't consider Rickard of bad character just because he had once run a gambling house, "no more than I would say a man who runs a church is necessarily of good character."

The jury was out ten minutes and returned with a verdict of not guilty.

Rickard returned to the business of promoting fights. Dempsey and Kearns took on the fight with Gibbons in Shelby, Montana. It was a financial failure, and Tex must have smiled. Casting around for a colorful foe for Dempsey, he came up with Luis Angel Firpo, the Argentinian.

"Why, boy," Tex told Hype Igoe, a sportswriter, "him and Dempsey will make the greatest fight you ever seed." Igoe said that this time Rickard was wrong, and Tex merely nodded and said we'll see.

Some time before this bout, Rickard had advised Dempsey not to take Firpo lightly—but just before fight time he visited Jack and asked him to go easy on "this poor dub." "He's slow and moves like an old tub," Rickard said.

"Go to hell," Jack said calmly.

The Rickard magic was still intact. The crowd at the Polo Grounds on September 14, 1923, totaled 88,228 persons, who paid $1,127,882—all this with the mandatory New York State limit of $27.50 as a top ticket price. The fight was a wild and woolly classic, even though Dempsey knocked out Firpo as early as the second round. James Crusinberry of the Chicago *Tribune* said the first was "the greatest round of battling since the Silurian Age," with seven knockdowns, including the one in which Dempsey slipped through the ropes and fell into the crowd.

BY NOW PRESIDENT of the Madison Square Garden Corporation, Rickard was the driving force behind the building of the new Garden, on Eighth Avenue between Forty-ninth and Fiftieth Streets, in 1925. It opened in November with a six-day bicycle race, and for the next forty-three years was the most famous sports arena in the world.

Sadly for Rickard, his Edith Mae died of a heart ailment in October, just before the Garden opened.

In September of 1926, Tex staged the Dempsey-Tunney bout in the Sesquicentennial Stadium in Philadelphia; 120,757 persons paid $1,895,723, the greatest such figures of all time up to then.

The result of the fight depressed Rickard, who was very close to Dempsey by this time. "I can hardly believe it," he said, sitting in his hotel suite later that damp night. "I never thought it could happen to him."

Someone asked him what he would do now.

"I dunno," he said slowly. "This other feller ain't never been a drawing card. Dempsey was the one who drew them in."

CHAPTER 8

THE WORLD STILL was spinning furiously in those early days of 1927.

Earl Carroll lost an appeal in United States Circuit Court after having been convicted of testifying falsely in a lower court, and was sentenced to a year and a day in a federal penitentiary. On Washington's Birthday in 1926, Mr. Carroll had given his famous party onstage at the *Vanities* theatre. He had originally been charged with violating the liquor laws, but he put his foot into it when he testified in court that the party had never taken place.

At a dinner in New York's Commodore Hotel, Senator-elect Robert F. Wagner launched a campaign to nominate Al Smith for the Presidency, and in Montreal seventy-seven children died when a slight fire started a ten-minute panic during the showing of a movie, *Get 'Em Young.* In Fergus Falls, Minnesota, a barbershop porter named Gus Comstock won back his national coffee-drinking title by swallowing 85 cupfuls in seven hours and fifteen minutes (a Texan had drunk 71 and beaten Gus's old mark of 62), but he developed a slight fever and couldn't reach his goal of 100. And, perhaps most absorbing, Peaches Heenan sued Daddy Browning for separation.

Daddy was Edward W. Browning, who said he was fifty-two and looked older, resembling Foxy Grandpa. A lover of the spotlight—and of young girls—he was divorced by his first wife because of "his penchant for flappers," and early in 1926 he met and married fifteen-year-old Frances Belle Heenan, called "Peaches." It was Peaches of whom Runyon wrote, "I hesitate to expatiate on so delicate a matter, but her legs are what the boys call piano legs." Everything Browning did was to the accompaniment of newspaper publicity, including the practical jokes he played on Peaches and his habit of jumping out from behind doors and crying "Woof! Woof!" at her. It was a lovely, foolish, harmless, ridiculous story, and the tabloids, notably the *Graphic,* went to town on it. It even precipitated circulation battles, and on one occasion *Mirror* delivery men hijacked batches of *Graphics* and threw them into the East River.

As Dorothy Parker wrote, life was a glorious cycle of song, "a medley of extemporanea."

RICKARD STILL kept after Dempsey. On January 9 he sent a wire to Los Angeles to find out when and if Jack would return to New York, and Tex told the reporters that Dempsey would not be coming back to fight "for the money he can make out of it. He has all the money he wants or ever will need." On the West Coast, Dempsey said he was going to do some light training and see what was what. And from Philadelphia's Mayor Kendrick came one of the first bids for the next title bout, "or at least one of the elimination fights."

Dempsey then went daily for a few days to the Manhattan Gymnasium in Los Angeles, spending hours running, punching the bag and sparring lightly. Tunney, meanwhile, had a disagreement with his theatrical promoters and returned to New York from Minneapolis for several days to clear it up. Actually he was in Manhattan more than a day before the papers knew of it, and *Times* sports columnist John Kieran chided him gently, saying that when a heavyweight champion came to town, "bands should play, fight fans should cheer and flashlight pictures should be taken in all directions." Kieran also commented *en passant* that for Dempsey to get back into genuine condition, "he would have to work harder than any day laborer, harder than any steel puddler."

Ring magazine asked Rickard to rank the heavyweights of the day, and, in order, he named Tunney, Dempsey, Sharkey, Delaney, Berlenbach, Paolino and Maloney. Paolino? He was a thick-set, beetle-browed Basque of remarkable endurance and not too much skill who apparently had publicity-conscious aides. A report came from Cuba that the Basque had killed three wild boar there singlehanded, shooting one, clubbing another and killing the third with his bare fists, but it developed later that the locale had been Tampa, Florida, and that the wild boar were razorback hogs, whose farmer-owner

Jack Dempsey at twenty-two, just a year away from Maumee Bay, near Toledo, Ohio, and the heavyweight championship of the world.

"The magnificent rube." Tex Rickard, boxing's greatest promoter, in 1920, with his five million-dollar gates still before him.

What a fight crowd used to look like. At Boyle's 30 Acres, Jersey City, on July 2, 1921, seventy-seven thousand watched the Dempsey-Carpentier fight, the first of the financially fabulous fights of the Twenties.

"Don't kill him, Jack," Rickard had pleaded—but Dempsey didn't listen. Here he measures Carpentier before the knockout.

In an unexpectedly tough title fight, Dempsey (r.) outpointed Tommy Gibbons in 1923, reminding one and all that he knew how to box as well as slug. The bout was held in Shelby, Montana.

Two years later—1925—and just a year away from Philadelphia and glory, Gene Tunney knocked out Gibbons in the twelfth round of their battle at the Polo Grounds.

The most famous knockdown in ring history. Seven punches have landed, Tunney is falling—and the long count is about to begin, in the seventh round of the Chicago fight, September 1927.

ABOVE: *Twelve, thirteen—how many?—seconds have gone by. Dave Barry counts as Tunney, his eyes clear once again, waits for the count to reach its end. Dempsey has finally gone to a neutral corner, but his moment has come and gone, not to come again.* BELOW: *Dempsey goes down in the eighth of the same fight—and, ironically, referee Dave Barry, not waiting for Tunney to go to a neutral corner, begins a count that, fortunately, will be brief.*

The days of wine and roses. Dempsey, the champion, supervises Rudolph Valentino's boxing lesson with Gene Delmont in Hollywood.

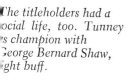

The titleholders had a social life, too. Tunney s champion with George Bernard Shaw, ght buff.

"The fighting Marine," he was called. A thoughtful, logical, reasoning fighter, Tunney is shown here on his way to his two dates with destiny in Philadelphia and Chicago.

demanded and got payment for them.

Paolino was to last for some time, finally sliding into obscurity much later when he fought a young Negro named Joe Louis. Crouched over, Paolino didn't let a punch land on him until a few rounds had passed, but when he erred and looked up from his bent-over position Louis caved in the side of his face with one punch.

From Europe came a challenge from Phil Scott, the British heavyweight champion, who had just beaten the Italian titleholder, Bartazzolo. Unfortunately Scott had already become known as "Fainting Phil" because of his penchant for swooning when struck anywhere near the beltline. Berlenbach seemed to be removed from consideration when Mike McTigue, the Irishman, knocked him out in four rounds at the Garden.

McTigue was no more than an average-sized light-heavyweight, but Rickard was missing no bets. He signed Mike to fight Sharkey on March 3 at the Garden. From the New York State branch of the American Legion came a petition asking that Tunney's title defense be held before September 10, 1927, since the Legion was holding a convention in Paris and it hoped to have Tunney there. The tenth would be, for this purpose, the last date on which Gene could fight before sailing for Europe.

Malone went to Paris for a visit, and there was an indication that he had taken over at least some of Gibson's responsibilities with Tunney. The cherubic attorney said he had the right to arrange a bout for the champion in Europe "provided the purse is big enough."

Dempsey still wasn't out of the woods. On Monday, February 7, *The New York Times* had a page-one story that the former champion was seriously ill with blood poisoning and "may never fight again."

It may not have been quite that omnious, but there was no doubt Dempsey was at least painfully ill. He had first noticed a slight scratch on the middle finger of his left hand while on a motor trip to San Francisco with Estelle, and in the days immediately following, infection spread rapidly.

His left hand and arm were swollen to twice their normal size, and Dr. Warren Clark of Hollywood Hospital operated on them six times in eighteen hours. Jack lost twelve pounds in three days, existed only on fruit juice, got no sleep and had day and night nurses at his home applying fresh dressings every fifteen minutes. Dr. Clark said he seemed to be beating his illness, but hedged with the announced possibility that "the infection has gained such headway that its spread might not be stopped."

Ill as he was, Jack got some small good news; his three-year-old gelding, Old Kickapoo, campaigning in Estelle's racing colors, won the El Domingo Handicap at Tijuana.

The heavyweight title picture continued to change this way and that. Berlenbach, after his defeat by McTigue, quit the ring to enter the lumber business. On Friday, February 18, Delaney dropped out of the competition when Jim Maloney beat him easily in ten rounds at the Garden before 20,000 fans.

Twenty thousand fans for a non-title bout at the Garden. It was average. Going to the Friday-night fights at the big new Eighth Avenue arena was a ritual with many.

In Tacoma, Washington, Tunney was asked about the opponent situation, and he said the leading contenders seemed to be Sharkey and Maloney but "I'm quite certain neither can defeat me." Dempsey, he conceded, still was in the running "but he hasn't made his position known yet."

In Washington State, legislators were trying to push through a bill to legalize boxing, and they invited Gene to address their legislature so boxing's enemies there could see "an ideal, clean-living boxer." In turn, Gene proclaimed Governor R. H. Hartley and Al Smith "the greatest men since Lincoln" and expressed a desire to live someday in the wonderful state of Washington.

IN AN AUDITORIUM on the shore of Lake Michigan, the Chicago Civic Opera Company did the third act of *Faust*. Through a broadcast marred only slightly by static, twenty-five radio stations linked with thirteen thousand miles of telephone wire transmitted the performance to an estimated ten million persons, more than had ever heard an opera at one time. From New York's Park Avenue Association came word that the residents of that avenue between Thirty-fourth and Ninety-sixth Streets averaged $75,000 in annual income a year, and that the four thousand families in the area spent $280,000,000 dollars a year. A hurricane struck Great Britain from the Scilly Isles to Edinburgh out of season, and eight were killed in Glasgow alone.

The famous $6,000,000 home of Senator William A. Clark, the Montana copper king, at Seventy-seventh Street and Fifth Avenue in Manhattan, was sold for less than $3,000,000. Myrtle Huddleston, a Long Beach, California, woman who had been swimming less than a year (she took it up to lose weight), survived a barracuda bite to become the first female to swim the Catalina Channel. En route to Saint Augustine, Florida, in his private railroad car, former Senator Chauncey M. Depew chided Thomas Edison for having said, at eighty, that the word "God" had no meaning for him. And along Broadway, detectives raided the plays *Sex, The Captive* and *The Virgin Man* and arrested forty-one actors for giving immoral performances, including Basil Rathbone, Helen Menken and Mae West.

ON SUNDAY, February 20, Rickard posted a second $100,000 to bind his contract with Tunney and announced that the heavyweight situation would have to await further clarification until McTigue fought Sharkey.

Dempsey, his blood poisoning almost gone, started to do some roadwork in Los Angeles but had nothing new to say. "Perhaps in two or three weeks," he commented, "I'll be able to say whether I'll continue boxing or retire."

Rickard, meanwhile, was looking ahead. Confident of Dempsey's ability, and contemplating two big bouts for the year instead of one, he said a little pompously that Jack would have to fight at least one other contender or "receive scant consideration" for a second Tunney bout. His idea, he mused, was to have Dempsey face the winner of his elimination series, the victor to box Tunney.

Sharkey blew in from Boston once more, as breezy as ever, to train at Stillman's for McTigue, and another contender dropped by the wayside when Knut Hansen was decisioned by Paolino at the Garden.

Fugazy, still trying, reportedly offered Dempsey $300,000 to box Maloney at the Polo Grounds in the spring, but Rickard countered this by saying he was planning to match Maloney with Paolino in the Garden in May.

IN SHANGHAI, labor unions began striking. The police arrested many of the leaders and beheaded at least twenty of them, hanging their heads from poles afterward. In Chicago, William Hale ("Big Bill") Thompson was nominated for mayor on the Republican ticket in a primary marked by shootings, sluggings, thefts of ballot boxes, police raids and the arrests of two hundred gangsters and vote-repeaters. On the West Coast, Babe Ruth, just finished making a movie, said flatly he would hold out for a two-year contract with the New York Yankees at $100,000 a year (he settled finally for $210,000 for three years). In Paris a heavy guard was thrown around the American Embassy after the Ambassador received letters saying he would be killed if the anarchists Sacco and Vanzetti were executed in Massachusetts.

ON FRIDAY, March 4, there was big news from Rickard on several fronts. He announced plans to expand or build sports arenas in Philadelphia, Detroit and Pittsburgh (including a $5,000,000 layout in Philadelphia) and a definite bid to purchase the controlling interest in a New York ball club. It was reported that Tex had offered Colonel Jacob Ruppert $4,000,000 for the Yankees but had been turned down and then had bid $2,500,000, again unsuccessfully, for the Giants.

The same night, the aging McTigue fell out of the heavyweight jigsaw puzzle when Sharkey won a technical knockout over him in twelve rounds. The result didn't boost Sharkey's stock. The balding Irishman had been well ahead on points before fatigue caught up with him.

In San Francisco, Tunney pronounced another judgment: Dempsey, he thought, was "far superior to any of the present heavyweight title contenders." He said he would be back in the East in mid-March and then would head for the Adirondack Mountains to start leisurely training for the long summer ahead.

Trouble continued to plague Dempsey. In Hollywood six physicians recommended that he enter a hospital for an operation at the base of his spine, which, they believed, would clear up his blood-poisoning problems. Jack evidently had been bothered this way before, and in 1926 alone had allegedly had three outbreaks of such an infection, the first in Atlantic City just before the Tunney bout.

The trouble apparently had originated in a fight six or seven years before when Dempsey, knocked down, had chipped a bone at the base of his spine. Gradually a friction point developed in the area and the chronic infection began. An operation in New York City five years before had not cleared it up.

"I realize that the doctors know their business," Jack said glumly, "but I had got all set to open a training camp in the woods within a week. I feel fine."

Rickard kept after Jack. He wired him a proposal to fight Paolino and then the winner of a Sharkey-Maloney bout. The pickings would be comparatively small, Tex said—$250,000 for the two fights—but Jack would be able to find out if he was ready for Tunney. Or if he was through.

CHAPTER 9

As MARCH came in, Henry Morgenthau, the former Ambassador to Turkey, wrote to a Washington correspondent of the *Berliner Tagenblatt* that "the dark shadows of monarchism had passed forever from Germany" and German nationals were finding at last "the absolute relief to every freedom of thought and speech." In the Transvaal, South Africa, 25,000 persons, some Olympic athletes, raced across the Grasfontein Farm to stake claims in diamond fields, and in Washington the United States Supreme Court held unconstitutional a Texas law barring Negroes from voting in a Democratic primary election. Justice Holmes read the opinion on the eve of his eighty-sixth birthday. George H. Doran published *The Seven Pillars of Wisdom* in America, but there were just twenty-two copies . . . and only ten of these were available to the public at $20,000 a copy. Doran said neither he nor Lawrence really was anxious to sell copies of the original book, and the high price was "for the paradoxical purpose of suppressing the full text." Lawrence—unheard of for a year and reportedly now a mechanic in the British Tank Corps in India with the rank of private—wanted to prevent "the full story" of his adventures from becoming public property. For the poor general public, a shortened edition to be called *Revolt in the Desert* was planned.

IN CALIFORNIA, Jack Dempsey made his move.

He called a press conference and said that he would go to Wheeler Hot Springs, seventy-five miles north of Los Angeles, and set up a training camp in the mountains to rough it for several weeks, hiking, tree chopping and, ultimately, rounding up some sparring partners and working out. Gus Wilson, one of his loyal trainers, would accompany him, he said—and he wasn't going to go through with the operation the six physicians had recommended.

"If I can come back," Dempsey said, "and I think I can, I'm ready to fight any man they want to put up, if the purse is right. I'm hardly financially independent, but I'll never fight as a ham-and-egger." He added that he wasn't tied up with any promoter and he had no immediate bouts under consideration.

For the first time Dempsey admitted that he "wasn't right" for the Tunney fight in 1926—but it had nothing to do with poisoned coffee or anything like that. "A lot of things published about my bad condition were all bunk," he said, "but it is a fact that I was stale. I went stale a full week before the big bout and I couldn't snap out of it. Each day I thought I would do all right the next, but I didn't.

"I simply couldn't get started—and Gene got to me first."

Jack added that when his sparmates "edged in on me" during training, he knew that somehow something was wrong. "Now," he finished up, "I'm out to see if I can get back to where I was."

John Kieran wrote a *Times* piece after the announcement in which he pointed out that "a year's vacation can do more harm to a prizefighter than half a dozen blows to the point of a rugged chin." He cautioned even Dempsey's most fervent admirers not to forget that Tunney had great pride even though "it is said Tunney takes no great pride in being heavyweight champion. He is in it for the money."

Tunney took the news of Dempsey's emergence with no public comment. As for himself, he said, he planned to sail for Europe in mid-May for a month and would box an exhibition in London around May 30, a few days before the Derby at Epsom Downs. He finished up his vaudeville tour in San Diego and then boxed some exhibitions in Denver and Cleveland before returning to the East. He also found time to present a forty-five-pound English bulldog to the Marine Corps to replace Sergeant Major Jiggs, the Corps mascot that had just died.

Along the boxing front, there was a report that trustees of the Garden were trying to get Rickard to confine his activities to New York City and that his great plans for development elsewhere were collapsing slowly. And in the one important fight of the month, Paolino won a split decision over Tom Heeney, a durable young Australian, at the Garden.

FOR THE REST of March and in the early days of April, Cauliflower Row was comparatively quiet. Or, perhaps more to the point, the nation for once had more serious things to which to turn its attention.

China, for instance, had been smoldering, bubbling and erupting, and now, on March 25, the Chinese Nationalists entered Nanking and assaulted many foreigners, including the British, American and Japanese consuls. For a day or two the fate of 155 Americans was unknown. There may have been no connection, but almost simultaneously tong wars broke out in Chicago, Brooklyn, Newark, Cleveland and Pittsburgh, after two years' peace. The Leong and Hip Sing tongs had at each other, and once again police patrolled the "bloody angle" at New York's Doyers and Pell Streets. Shortly thereafter both the Americans and the British threatened to shell Nanking, and their citizens were freed by the Nationalists.

But there was other violence to come.

On Saturday, April 9, Judge Webster Thayer in Dedham, Massachusetts, sentenced Nicola Sacco and Bartolomeo Vanzetti to die in the electric chair during the week of July 10. The two men were Italian-born, Sacco a shoemaker and Vanzetti a fish peddler. They had been arrested in the spring of 1920 for alleged complicity in a $15,776.52 payroll robbery in South Braintree, Massachusetts, in which a paymaster and a factory guard were killed.

Although in subsequent trials the prosecution offered sixty-one witnesses who placed Sacco and Vanzetti at the scene of the crime, it seemed that there were large, definite gaps in the evidence presented, and intellectuals and pseudo-intellectuals throughout America and all over the world rallied to the defense of the two immigrants.

The arguments and furor seemed to revolve chiefly around Judge Thayer, a fifty-seven-year-old jurist who, regardless of his qualifications, undoubtedly was bigoted and inflammatory. As one of his acquaintances said, "I could not say that I think he is at all times a bad man or that he is a confirmed wicked man. But I say that he is a narrow-minded man; he is full of prejudice; he is carried away with his fear of Reds. . . ."

There seemed little doubt that, as reported, he asked friends in private, "Did you see what I did to those anarchist bastards?" and said that he had "got those damn Reds good and proper" (Robert Benchley, *Life*'s drama critic, testified to these statements in an affidavit). *The Boston Globe*'s courtroom reporter, Frank P. Sibley, said that Judge Thayer's charge to the jury was astonishing. "His whole manner, his whole attitude," Sibley wrote, "seemed to be that the jurors were there to convict these two men."

The jury took seven hours to convict Sacco and Vanzetti, and in the immediate years that followed, their case was pleaded before the public by Edna St. Vincent Millay, John Dos Passos, Dorothy Parker, Heywood Broun and many others. Much later—indeed, after the execution—Maxwell Anderson was to write a poetic, searing drama, *Winterset*—his greatest play—in which there was a judge, obviously patterned after Thayer, who went from person to person, dazedly claiming he had done the right thing in sending the reported anarchists to their death.

In the years following the conviction, such persons as Mussolini, George Bernard Shaw, Romain Rolland and John Galsworthy asked for clemency for the two men. One night at an American Legion meeting in Syracuse, New York, Gene Tunney declared, "Radicalism must be suppressed and the Legion can help in suppressing it!" He did not mention Sacco and Vanzetti by name, but listeners drew their own conclusions.

Early in April a speech by Herbert Hoover in Washington was rather crudely televised to New York City by the Bell Laboratories of the American Telephone and Telegraph Company. A story from Washington stated that 82 percent of the nation had paid no income tax in 1926, and that 207 persons had paid taxes on incomes of a million dollars or more.

The country was prospering. From the Clock Manufacturers Association of America came word that the average workingman made a cent and a half a minute, while President Coolidge earned fifty cents a minute and Gloria Swanson, the movie performer, $7.40. When "all the mass" of workers wasted one second, $9980 was lost.

In Shanghai, Chiang Kai-shek had a hundred Communists executed—the chief of the seamen's union was beheaded without trial—but Chiang's followers embarrassed him by pledging their friendship to Russia. In Hollywood, Charlie Chaplin agreed to pay a million dollars owed in back taxes for a five-year period. Actor Paul Kelly was arrested and imprisoned for several years for beating to death a man named Ray Raymond after he,

Kelly, had admitted loving Raymond's wife, former Broadway star Dorothy Mackaye. In New York, Mae West's case came up for trial, and she was fined $500 and sentenced to ten days in jail for giving an obscene performance in *Sex*.

DEMPSEY CONTINUED light training and Tunney continued touring. On Wednesday, April 20, Tunney returned to New York and breakfasted with sportswriters in his seventh-floor suite at the Hotel Breslin on Twenty-ninth Street—the hotel entrance was decorated with American flags and bunting—and said that he expected his fall opponent to be Dempsey, after perhaps a bout between Jack and the elimination-tournament survivor.

Gene also reported that when he had appeared with his touring act in Los Angeles, Gus Wilson and Jerry the Greek had come backstage (they said they had been in the audience to study Tunney's boxing for Dempsey) and told him that Dempsey was in excellent condition and, at several entertainments in his honor, "never missed a dance."

Tunney looked good. At 191 pounds, about four or five over his fighting weight, he somehow looked much heavier, more mature. He said he had been playing a good deal of golf and that 92 had been his last score. After the breakfast he shook hands with a number of schoolboys and spoke to them in "his characteristic measured words and sentences," according to one newsman. Billy Gibson still was around, and he said it was likely that Gene's European trip would be canceled and that the champion would undoubtedly vacation at a mountain resort in the early summer.

Fugazy was still at it. On Friday, April 22, he announced he had bought property in the West Fifties in New York from the Hearst interests for $1,325,000 and would build a $12,000,000 sports arena there. And he scored a minor victory by taking the Pete Latzo-Joe Dundee welterweight championship match away from Rickard, scheduling it for June 3.

Several weeks of roughing it and light training pepped Dempsey up. He had been chopping wood and hauling it, running and working out briskly, and he reported that he had melted off eleven pounds and weighed an even 200. Now he was working with both the light and heavy bags and also shadowboxing, and he decided to move his headquarters to Sober's Ranch in the Ventura Mountains near Ojai, California.

"I've gotten out from under the strain that must wear down a champion," Dempsey said. "Now all I have to do is fight. Tunney can do the worrying. If I meet him again, I will regain the heavyweight championship. If the fight world thinks I should take on some warming-up fights, I will do it."

At this point there seemed little doubt Jack was planning to come back if he could. Gus Wilson prepared to head eastward to confer with Rickard and to dig up some sparmates for Dempsey.

When did Jack think he might be ready?

"Around July 4," he said.

Rickard had been spending a few days in Florida. He returned, deeply tanned, and was asked at a press conference if he already had Dempsey and Tunney signed for a return fight. Tex shrugged.

"I don't very well see how I can match them," he said,

"unless Sharkey and Maloney are so bad in their coming encounter that the public won't support either in a title fight." The Sharkey-Maloney bout already had been made—and, Rickard added, he wasn't counting out Paolino.

"If he [Dempsey] can't beat Paolino," Rickard said, "he might just as well quit the ring."

A few days later, after talking with Gus Wilson, Rickard said it was his plan at the moment to have two qualifying bouts for a Tunney opponent: Dempsey would box Paolino, and the winner of that bout would meet the Maloney-Sharkey victor.

Gene Normile, who had managed Dempsey for the Philadelphia match, came to New York, checked in at the Belmont and let it be known that he now was simply Jack's business manager and that Dempsey was "attending to his own ring business." He said that the former champion was in high spirits. On the Coast the old boxing master Leach Cross wrote a friend in New York that Jack would "make a sensational comeback."

The drums were beginning to roll. The public was rolling up its sleeve for the hypodermic needle. Rickard smiled and rubbed his hands as the ballyhoo started, slowly but surely. Of course, there were a number of cynics around who said that Rickard simply was spoofing the public with his "tournament" and that Tex all the while was figuring on a Dempsey-Tunney bout and, indeed, had it all set.

Regardless of who was to fight Tunney in September, however, there remained the problem of where to stage the contest. New York would have been ideal except for one large problem: the price limit on tickets for any fight there was $27.50, and there didn't seem much likelihood it would be changed. Rickard couldn't see this. He had visions of a $100 top for the next big bout, and when he let this be known, Chicago stepped in.

A group of Chicago businessmen proposed to Rickard that he hold the bout in Grant Park, with its sprawling layout on the shores of Lake Michigan, where a big new stadium, Soldier's Field, had been erected. It would seat up to 150,000 persons, they pointed out, and there would be the possibility of the first $2,000,000 gate in history. "We'll promote it ourselves," the syndicate said, "or we'll split the venture fifty-fifty with Rickard."

APRIL SPED along. Dr. Henry F. Osborn, president of the American Museum of Natural History, was quoted as saying flatly that man had not descended from the apes but, rather, had sprung sixteen million years before from a stock "neither human nor apelike." Up at the 102nd Engineers Armory in New York's Washington Heights section, sailors from the fleet in town on its annual visit crowded around a ring to watch Gene Tunney referee some bouts. Fugazy staged a light-heavyweight–heavyweight bout at Ebbets Field in Brooklyn, where 20,000 fans shivered on a cool evening as a couple of flashy boxers, Tommy Loughran and Young Stribling (later to die in a motorcycle accident), put on a dazzling exhibition. Loughran won.

Tunney was in and around New York quite a bit, still relaxing before going into light training. A number of his afternoons were spent with George Luks, a well-known portrait artist who had been commissioned to paint his picture. Tunney and Luks went frequently to art galleries on Fifth Avenue, where the champion was visibly staggered when told the price of a sunset by Monet.

Dempsey wired Rickard he would be in New York for discussions on May 16, but his message was regarded skeptically. Illness and other problems had forced him to change previous plans from time to time, and the boxing writers were beginning to think a jinx was hovering over his shoulder.

Rickard, like Tunney, still was palling around with the Right People. On Monday night, May 16, he was given a dinner at the Commodore Hotel attended by Mayors Walker of New York and Hague of Jersey City, as well as Walter Chrysler, Charles M. Schwab, Colonel John S. Hammond, Condé Nast, Bernard Gimbel and Thomas Hitchcock, Jr., the polo star. Jimmy Walker presented Tex with a three-foot-high English silver-and-mahogany plaque lauding him as a "master of his craft."

Rickard, for once, had little to say, except to note that he had heard from Dempsey, who had advised him that he would not be in condition "or of a mind" for a fight before August, and Tex had therefore abandoned plans for a Dempsey-Paolino bout.

The sports beat continued busily. The Saturday before Rickard's dinner, Harry Payne Whitney's Whiskery nipped Osmand at the wire in the fifty-third Kentucky Derby, with Pony McAtee riding the winner, and on Thursday, May 19, the fourth bout between Sharkey and Maloney was scheduled for Yankee Stadium. Rain forced its postponement until the following night, however . . . and by then, although at least 40,000 persons filled the Stadium for the fight, another news event had crowded it off the front pages.

135

CHAPTER 10

T H E *Spirit of St. Louis* took off from Roosevelt Field on Long Island at 7:52 a.m. on Friday, May 20. The field was muddy, as the all-night rain had continued into morning. The plane had 451 gallons of gasoline aboard, and it just barely cleared a line of high-tension wires.

Lindbergh was on his way.

The *Spirit* was a little, silver, single-engined airplane manufactured by the Ryan Company, and its destination was Europe in general and Paris in particular. Its pilot, an airmail flyer named Charles Lindbergh, was attempting something that never had been done: to fly across the Atlantic Ocean alone.

There seemed a general element of surprise at Lindbergh's departure in the murky Long Island morning. He had been in New York for a few days, waiting to go, but still the public was a little startled at his seemingly sudden take-off. It shouldn't have been.

Earlier in the year a $25,000 prize had been put up by Raymond Orteig, the owner of New York's Hotel Brevoort, for the first man or crew to fly non-stop to Paris. A handful of famous aviators, including Commander Richard E. Byrd, Clarence Chamberlin, Bert Acosta and two French war aces, Nungesser and Coli, had been considered favorites in the race. But Lindbergh had filed his notice of entry as far back as March 1.

Nungesser and Coli were first off the mark, on May 8, taking the east-to-west route. The next night the Paris *L'Intransigéant* published an extra, saying the airmen had landed at New York at 4:35 a.m. Paris time. The French, particularly in Paris, where a lighted signboard over the Place de l'Opéra announced the landing, went wild—prematurely. Nungesser and Coli were lost.

Byrd's triplane *America,* meanwhile, was being repaired after being damaged in a test flight. And at Curtiss Field, Chamberlin worked over his yellow single-engine plane, *Columbia.*

When Lindbergh flew into New York from San Diego in twenty-one hours and forty-five minutes, setting three records en route, the race became three-cornered.

The press called Lindbergh every trick name it could dream up—Lucky Lindy, Slim, Lindy . . . and the most absurd, The Flying Fool. There was nothing foolish or chancy about what he was doing. He was taking a calculated risk, of course; he was being extremely daring. But within that context, he kept risk to a minimum. Lindbergh could fly, he could navigate, he was intelligent and he was sane.

He was also slender, grinning and a practical joker. His constant companion during the week or so he spent in New York was Richard Blythe, a publicist for Wright Whirlwind, the company that had made the engine for the *Spirit*. Blythe was awakened one morning by Lindbergh tossing a pitcher of ice water on him. Another morning he awoke and found the flyer straddling him trying to shave off his mustache.

For days Lindbergh, fretting, had waited for a favorable weather report for his crossing. On the night of May 19, Blythe and he were heading for dinner at the Newspaper Club in West Forty-second Street, planning to go from there to see the Broadway musical *Rio Rita*. Driving in New York's wet streets, Lindbergh suggested a call to the Weather Bureau. Blythe made the call and, when he came back, said, "No dinner and no show tonight, Slim. You've got your weather."

"Right," Lindbergh said. "We'll go back to the field."

His plane was then at Curtiss Field. He went to his room at the Garden City Hotel, hoping for three hours or so of sleep, but, lying in bed, he found himself wide awake. Not worrying, really. Thinking. He went over and over his plans in his head and at last, before 3:00 a.m., he returned to Curtiss Field and had his plane towed by the tail to Roosevelt Field.

When he climbed into the cockpit at 7:40, he had in his flying suit letters of introduction, including one to Ambassador Myron Herrick, and, reportedly, a letter of credit for a single return passage on the Cunard Line.

Heavily laden with fuel, the *Spirit* trundled down the runway and twice got out of the mud and became airborne, only to drop back again. Finally its forward progress reached sixty miles an hour and it got up to stay, over the trees and high-tension wires. It headed due east.

"The suspense of it, the daring of it, the triumph and glory of it, these are the stuff that makes immortal news," a *Times* editorial said. And the *New York Sun* said, "Alone? Is he alone at whose right side rides Courage, with Skill within the cockpit and Faith upon the left? . . . Alone? With what other companions would that man fly to whom the choice were given?"

THERE WERE somewhere between 40,000 and 70,000 persons in Yankee Stadium on the night of May 20—no really accurate count was ever given out. All the talk— on the subways leading to the Bronx, outside the Stadium, in the limousines and taxis—was of Lindbergh.

It was one of Rickard's most elegant audiences, the front rows, as one reporter put it, "fairly groaning with millionaires." It was a chilly spring evening and overcoats had been broken out; there was only a handful of straw hats on the men. There was more than a sprinkling of dinner clothes and costly evening wraps, however. Around the ringside were Mortimer Schiff, Condé Nast, Herbert and Ralph Pulitzer, E. R. and W. Averell Harriman, Walter Chrysler, J. Cheever Cowdin, ten members of the Massachusetts Senate and fifty members of the Massachusetts House, not to mention half of the Boston City Council (both the fighters, Sharkey and Maloney, were Bostonians now).

Balding, illiterate, gravel-voiced Joe Humphreys, waving his hands again and again for silence from the huge crowd—there were no microphones, of course—announced at last that the Lone Eagle was three hundred miles at sea and on course. Then he asked for a moment of prayerful silence for Lindbergh, and the crowd rose. For a few seconds the Bronx was hushed. A voice from the stands bawled out, breaking the spell, "He's the greatest fighter of them all."

Then the fight crowd got down to the business at hand. It seemed apparent now that either of the fighters was only two bouts—perhaps only one—away from the big one. Paolino seemed to have been discarded. The Maloney-Sharkey winner undoubtedly would fight either Dempsey as a final obstacle, or Tunney himself for the title.

Maloney went into the ring as a 7-to-5 favorite. He was a false one. As the two neighborhood rivals fought for a $250,000 purse, Sharkey knocked Maloney down three times and then, in fifty-two seconds of the fifth round, knocked him out.

Sharkey was a trifle less boastful after the fight. "Maloney put up a great fight," he said. "I want Tunney. He's the next man for me. But if I have to, I'm ready to battle Dempsey." Johnny Buckley, his peppery manager, echoed Sharkey, adding that they weren't bound to fight for Rickard "but our future rests with him."

EDWIN L. JAMES's dispatch to *The New York Times* could not be improved upon:

"Lindbergh did it."

After more than thirty hours in the air, thirty long, endlessly long hours, many of them spent flying blind or skimming only a few hundred feet above the cresting North Atlantic, Lindbergh set his silver plane down at Le Bourget airfield outside Paris at 10:24 p.m. on Saturday, May 21.

A crowd of 25,000 had gathered in the darkness of the field, necessitating special police and two corps of fixed-bayonet soldiers. Now the crowd swept toward the plane, and its welcoming roar was deafening. Some said Lindbergh, sitting tiredly in the cockpit, said, "Well, I made it." Most felt he had said, "I am Charles Lindbergh," although later Lindbergh himself said he thought his first words were about his plane. He was afraid the mob would souvenir-hunt it into wreckage.

A couple of French pilots rescued him from the well-meaning crowd, slapped his flying cap on another American whom the Frenchmen mistook for Lindbergh, and spirited the hero to a darkened, empty hangar. He sat there is a small room, alone in his moment of triumph except for one of the French pilots, until he was escorted to a military official's office to await Ambassador Herrick, who arrived an hour later.

The French official, the two French pilots, Herrick and Lindbergh then drove to the American Embassy in Paris. They went by way of Place de l'Opéra and up the Champs-Elysées—where they stopped for a moment while Lindbergh, dazed and sleepy, got out and stood briefly at the tomb of the Unknown Soldier.

Back in New York, and across America, the natives went slightly mad. The *Times* had received ten thousand calls about Lindbergh in eleven hours, and at the suggestion of Mayor Walker, factory, ship and boat whistles blew steadily for five minutes, making a fantastic counterpoint to the sirens of every fire company in the city.

As the man said, Lindbergh did it.

ON SATURDAY, May 21, the two fighters dropped by Madison Square Garden and collected their paychecks from Rickard. Then Sharkey and his wife—who, as usual, hadn't seen him fight—began motoring back to Boston, while Maloney and Dan Carroll, his manager, took the train. "I must have been terrible," Maloney said sadly. Rickard then went to play golf with Billy Gibson.

Dempsey, always candid, said in Los Angeles after having heard the fight and read about it, "Sharkey is just about good enough to stop Tunney right now." He said that a fight between himself and Sharkey "should draw a big purse," but reported that Rickard had not yet made him a definite offer for a Sharkey bout. That surprised the fight crowd in New York City, since Rickard already had announced such a plan.

On Sunday, May 22, Rickard seemed to be playing it cool once more. "Now," he said meditatively, "I don't care whether Dempsey returns to the ring or not. I'm not short on material for a heavyweight title bout. If Dempsey does decide to return to the ring, he will have to meet Sharkey. There are no two ways about that."

Tunney seemed very much impressed by Sharkey's fast-boxing, crisp-hitting performance. "He is as good a fighter as I've ever seen," he said. "He has everything. I was really astonished at his showing. He's smarter than Dempsey and faster, though he's not as hard a hitter."

The *Times*'s expert, Dawson, master of the wrong guess, came out flatly and said it was likely that Sharkey, not Dempsey, would face Tunney in the autumn, with the bout undoubtedly being held in Philadelphia. "Sharkey may not be champion, but he will be in a few years or I miss my guess," Rickard said.

Tunney now was ready to begin light training. Originally he had favored Tom Luther's camp on the lake at

Saratoga Springs, New York, but for two reasons he decided instead to go to Speculator, New York. A camp there was run by Bill Osborne, an old wartime friend— Tunney had begun his 1926 training there. Secondly, there was no admission fee charged at his workouts. Tunney disliked making people pay to see him work.

Rickard pronounced his blessing on Gene as he left. "Tunney doesn't care whom he fights," Tex said. "As a matter of fact, he has no choice in the selection."

Tex is *said* to have said "whom."

THE LINDBERGH STORY dominated the front pages day after day. He received the Cross of the Legion of Honor from France, and 500,000 Frenchmen cheered him in the streets of Paris as he was en route to an official reception at the Hotel de Ville. *The New York Times* for four straight days carried the articles under a three-line, eight-column banner headline, the sort of treatment reserved ordinarily for the beginning or end of major wars. Lindy went to London; he was decorated by King George; he was offered the personal use of a cruiser for his return to Washington by Calvin Coolidge; he went to the English Derby. The world's hero wasn't a bird or a plane; it was Charles A. Lindbergh.

In Rome, a darker note. Speaking in the Chamber of Deputies, Benito Mussolini said that Italy would be able "to make her voice heard" between the coming years 1933 and 1940, by which time the nation would be able to mobilize a five-million-man army. Within those years, Il Duce added, Italy must be "fully prepared in a military sense for any critical point in European history."

Along Broadway the news was more vital to America.

Abie's Irish Rose, at the Republic Theatre, gave its 2151st performance and entered its sixth year.

TUNNEY LEFT for Speculator accompanied by his old friend Eddie Eagan and trainer Lou Fink. From the Midwest came the news that Dempsey's promoter pal Floyd Fitzsimmons was trying to schedule a Dempsey-Jack Delaney bout for Navin Field, the Detroit Tigers' ballpark. Dempsey, the tale went, had agreed to the fight.

Rickard smiled at the report and said he placed little stock in it. At a private dinner in the Biltmore Hotel honoring Tunney, who had turned thirty on May 25, and William Muldoon, the serio-comic chairman of the New York State Athletic Commission, Rickard repeated his feeling that Dempsey would be coming back only to salvage his honor.

"He isn't broke," Tex said. "It's impossible for a man who collected $719,000 less than a year ago to squander that sum in so short a time, and Dempsey has never been a spendthrift."

Tex reportedly had Paolino under an airtight contract, but on May 26 Fugazy, still picking up the crumbs, announced that he had signed the Basque to fight Harry Wills at the Polo Grounds on June 29. Rickard protested to the State Athletic Commission, but the group approved the bout, after which Tex said he might take it to the courts.

Chicago and Philadelphia businessmen kept after Rickard constantly, vying for the right to hold the championship bout in September. Johnny Buckley, Sharkey's manager, added a dollop of uncertainty to the whole thing when he came to New York for a talk with Rickard and told reporters that he had heard from "a particular friend" of Dempsey's that the old champion definitely would not return to the ring.

THE WORLD TURNED. In Newark, Shipwreck Kelly jockeyed a fifty-foot flagpole atop the Hotel St. Francis, trying to break his pole-sitting record of seven days and one hour. The Feds shut down Texas Guinan's Three Hundred Club and the raffish, almost masculine Texas promptly turned up on Broadway in a revue, *Padlocks of 1927,* with a singer, Lillian Roth, and a slick-haired dancer, George Raft. Fatty Arbuckle, the movie comic whose career had collided with a rape trial, lasted twelve performances onstage in *Baby Mine,* with a "Tennis, anyone?" actor named Bogart in the cast. Lizzie Borden, the onetime suspected ax murderess of her parents, died in Fall River, Massachusetts.

Big Bill Thompson was reelected mayor of Chicago and said he would try to have all references to England removed from the Chicago libraries. And on Saturday, June 4, Clarence Chamberlin and Charles A. Levine, "the millionaire junkman," took off from Roosevelt Field at 6:04 a.m. in their Bellanca monoplane *Columbia* for Europe. More particularly, their goal was either Berlin or Rome.

Bald and stocky, Levine was a strange figure, almost totally out of place in a plane cockpit. Yet, in a striped business suit, he was sitting next to Chamberlin as the yellow plane took off. His wife, noticing for the first time that her husband was making the chancy safari, fainted dead away. Just before take-off, Chamberlin scribbled a note and gave it to a reporter to relay to Lindbergh, who was due home in a few days: "Sorry not to wait to greet you, but I have the breaks in the weather, so I'm off."

Navigating solely by an old $50 magnetic compass—and getting lost now and then—Chamberlin was over the Atlantic in *Columbia* as Lindbergh sailed for the United States on the cruiser *Memphis*. On Monday, June 6, its gasoline gone after forty-two and a half hours in the air, the plane set down in the middle of a field near Eisleben, Germany, 110 miles southeast of Berlin. It had flown 4100 miles for a new distance record.

Refueled, *Columbia* set out on the final short leg to Berlin on Tuesday, June 7, but, having been stocked with only twenty gallons of fuel fetched from Eisleben, it had to make another forced landing sixty miles from Berlin. This second leg ended in comic-opera fashion as the monoplane dug into a muddy field and the propeller was broken at both ends. After the prop was mended, the plane made it to Tempelhof, the Berlin airport, where 150,000 Berliners greeted the bizarre pair.

Once again aviation took over the newspapers. Everything and anything pertaining to flying took precedence over all other news. In Berlin, Levine talked freely of starting a regular transatlantic service with multi-engined planes and said he would put $2,000,000 into the venture. The New York Stock Exchange closed its doors to honor living men for the second time in its history (the other had been when General John J. Pershing returned from France in 1919).

The *Memphis* brought Lindbergh into the Washington Navy Yard on Saturday, June 11. There were 37,000 telegrams plus three wagonloads of mail awaiting him. Newspaper advertisers turned their space over to welcoming Lindy. The United Cigar Stores had a full-page layout in the *Times,* with an eagle clutching a flag and the legend "America's New Eagle." In Potomac Park 300,000 persons, the largest crowd in the park's history, showed up to see President Coolidge pin the Flying Cross on the chest of Lindbergh at the foot of the Washington Monument.

IN CALIFORNIA, Dempsey made ready to break his wooded training camp. Buckley went out there to talk with Jack about fighting Sharkey and reported that Dempsey had said, "Sharkey and Tunney look alike to me; I'll fight anyone."

Rickard tentatively penciled in the fight for July 21 at the Yankee Stadium and said both Dempsey and Sharkey would get 25 percent of the gate, just as Buckley, on the West Coast, was saying loudly that Sharkey wouldn't fight unless he got as much money as Dempsey. At the New York Navy Yard in Brooklyn, 5000 sailors heard Sharkey, attending amateur bouts there, say, "Join the Navy, take a good-natured punch at your bunkmate— and become wealthy."

The old order passed. On Thursday, June 16, wreckers began tearing down the pine-bowl arena at Boyle's Thirty Acres in Jersey City, where six years earlier 77,000 persons had seen Dempsey and Carpentier.

The Dempsey-Sharkey deal, although not official, was wrapped up. Dempsey, heading east with Estelle, was ready for it, and Buckley accepted terms for Sharkey. In Houston en route, Jack said he would show the public the Dempsey "they used to know," and in New York, Rickard began to be flooded with ticket applications, although the two fighters had not yet signed for the newsreel cameras.

Rickard moved ahead with his plans. He decided on a $27.50 top price for seats, the most the New York law would allow, and he looked for a $1,250,000 gate, providing 60,000 fans attended. Minimum seat price was set at $3.30. Gus Wilson checked into New York and went around to Stillman's Gym on the prowl for sparmates for Dempsey; a couple of days later he went horse-playing at the Aqueduct track—and said he tentatively had booked Tom Luther's training camp at Lake Saratoga for the old champion. "I'm here in connection with Dempsey's racing interests," he added stiffly.

Dempsey's train stopped at Atlanta and Washington on the way east and reporters noted that he both looked and sounded good. In Atlanta he declared he admired Sharkey's confidence, "but he doesn't frighten me." "While Tunney beat me, I was not myself that night," Jack said. "I know I have a lot of fight and a lot of hard punches left in me." A great crowd greeted him in Wilmington, Delaware, when he and Estelle left the train and went to Miss Taylor's mother's house for the night, and Dempsey, turning cagey, said that if he couldn't close a deal with Rickard, he had three other bouts in view, one to be promoted in San Francisco by the old fighter Willie Ritchie.

CHAPTER 11

Dempsey returned to New York City on Wednesday, June 22, and agreed to fight Jack Sharkey on Thursday, July 21.

Still a little heavy, but looking fit, with his face a leathery brown from eleven weeks in the outdoors, he came to the Belmont Hotel after a seven-hour motor trip from Wilmington. Reporters had been tipped off and were crowded into the hotel lobby, but Dempsey wanted to see Rickard first; so he and his attorneys, Arthur F. Driscoll and Leonard Sachs, entered through the back way, striding through the kitchen and taking the rear elevator to Dempsey's suite, where Rickard was. He told Tex they had driven up to keep out of Pennsylvania, where Doc Kearns's legal suits still were pending.

They hassled about the terms for the Sharkey bout for a little while, but then agreement was reached and the newsmen were called in. Jack told them he had agreed to defend the title by September 1928 if he regained it from Tunney after defeating Sharkey. He would not disclose the percentage for which he had signed for the Sharkey bout. Reporters, who had heard talk of a 25–25 split with Sharkey, decided it was more likely Dempsey would receive 30 percent of the gate or a minimum of $250,000, and Sharkey would get 22.5 percent.

Dempsey had been denied a license to fight in New York before the Tunney match because he had dodged Harry Wills. He now said he would apply immediately for a new license and would head promptly for Saratoga to begin serious training. He added that his sparring partners already had been lined up by Gus Wilson and Jerry the Greek. They were, tentatively, Ray Neumann, Leo Lomski, Jack Gagnon, Carl Carter, Martin Burke and Bud Gorman (who had beaten Sharkey in 1925 and lost on a foul in a return bout a year later). Jimmy de Tarr, a West Coast friend of Jack's, would be along to handle the former champion's publicity.

Rickard was openly delighted with Dempsey's carefree manner and obvious fitness. "I think the fans will see a great fight," he said. "What is more, I'm sure a great crowd will see the fight." Rickard's chief, perhaps his only, interest in the bout was in its financial—and social —success; but he liked Dempsey, and if he had any leanings, and if it didn't make any difference to the fight's popularity, he probably wanted Jack to win.

And Dempsey *was* carefree. He led the newspaper and newsreel photographers to the roof, where he and Estelle posed for them until nearly dusk. One reporter asked him why he was coming back, and, grinning in the early-summer evening, he struck a melodramatic pose. "I'm fighting for glory," he said kiddingly.

More seriously, he said that money was a minor consideration. "I'm fighting because I want to fight," he said flatly. "It's my business. I'm not dead by a jugful. Because I was beaten doesn't mean I can't fight any more. These things happen. You have to lose a fight once in a while." He grinned again. "Particularly if you forget to duck one," he added.

He said he weighed 204, three pounds more than when he had quite training in California. Out of eighty-six active days at Ojai, he noted, he had boxed forty-five. He expected to meet Sharkey at 195 pounds.

Leaning against a parapet on the hotel roof, he looked out at the city's smoky, jagged skyline. "I don't know what was the matter in Philadelphia," he said candidly. "Maybe I had been away too long. I wasn't too good against Gibbons at Shelby, and I think Gibbons was as good a fighter as Tunney. But then I was better against Firpo.

"At any rate, I want to be convinced I'm wrong and that my ring days are positively over." He shrugged. "Maybe Sharkey can convince me."

ON THURSDAY, June 23, Edward, Prince of Wales, celebrated his thirty-third birthday in a pleasant manner. He and his brother George, dressed in Eton jackets with huge turned-down collars, pink bow ties and white socks, attended a costume party at the Duchess of Sutherland's home in London, where another guest, Winston Churchill, Chancellor of the Exchequer, attended as Henry the Eighth.

In New York City, Dempsey and Sharkey signed.

The ritual was supposed to have been held in Rickard's office at Madison Square Garden, but there was such a mob of newsmen, photographers and hangers-on that the ceremony was moved hurriedly to the ice rink on the roof of the Garden's Eighth Avenue side. Each man posted a $2500 forfeit and the terms were given out officially: 27.5 percent, or $275,000, for Dempsey; 22.5 percent for Sharkey.

For weeks the reporters had listened to the jaunty Sharkey going through his I'll-knock-them-all-dead routine, but this day they found him oddly quiet. Natty in a double-breasted tan suit, a checked light tan shirt, striped tie, tan shoes and a sailor straw with a dark green band, he kidded around a little and did an imitation of Rickard with his gold-headed cane, but was almost subdued when he posed for pictures with Dempsey. Perhaps for the first time he realized he was going into the ring with the man some had called the greatest fighter of all time.

Jack asked Sharkey about his wife, who was in the hospital, and the Bostonian mumbled something. His only audible remark to Dempsey was, "How's the weather, Jack?" to which Dempsey said firmly, "Warm." The sportswriters dutifully noted each syllable and even had some discussion about what color Dempsey's shirt was. Smoke-blue, they decided. When one was in on history in the making, accuracy was paramount.

Dempsey told reporters after the signing that he would dine with Rickard that evening and then leave that night for Saratoga with Estelle. He said he had engaged Leo P.

Flynn, a brisk, silver-haired old-timer who had managed Bud Gorman and Jack Renault, to be his business manager. The writers approved. Flynn was pure Cauliflower Row.

Buckley said Sharkey would train right in New York, at the Garden rink. First, however, he said, his boxer would take his wife out of the hospital and home to Boston on the morrow. Then he would go fishing for a week and start training for Dempsey on July 5. Dempsey left immediately by taxi and Sharkey walked across Forty-ninth Street, with a herd of small boys trailing him and hooting. He kidded them back and then flagged a cab when he reached Broadway.

COMMANDER BYRD's plans to fly the Atlantic still were being held up by bad weather, and in California, Dr. C. A. Wills said that his daughter Helen, the world's greatest amateur tennis player—perhaps a notch or two below the professional Suzanne Lenglen—had turned down an offer of $210,000 to star in a movie. "She'd turn it down if it were five hundred thousand," he added. In Massachusetts, Governor Fuller stayed the execution of Sacco and Vanzetti from July 10 to August 10, and in Honolulu, Naval Lieutenants Lester J. Maitland and Albert F. Hegenberger landed their plane at Hawaii after a twenty-six-hour flight from the United States, the first such in history.

Byrd and three crewmen, including the crack one-eyed pilot Bert Acosta, finally took off from Roosevelt Field for Paris on Wednesday, June 29, at 5:25 a.m. They had 250 letters aboard, including the first official airmail to Europe. One of the letters was from Mayor Walker to the

Lord Mayor of London.

The next day the nation waited breathlessly after Byrd radioed back that his tri-motored *America* was in dense fog and that he had seen no land or water for more than ten hours. His speed, he reported, was nearly 100 miles an hour. But finally, on Friday, July 1, the plane was nearly out of gas. Byrd calmly and wisely ditched it in the sea 200 meters from shore at Ver sur Mer, 120 miles from Paris. *America* had been in the air forty-three hours and twenty-one minutes. The plane was smashed, but all four flyers were safe, although Acosta suffered a fracture of the collarbone.

LEO FLYNN took charge in no uncertain style at Dempsey's camp in Saratoga, where a dark green five-room cottage was built for Jack on a country road set back from the lake and isolated from other buildings. Flynn and Jerry the Greek moved in there with Jack and Estelle.

Dempsey was thirty-two on Friday, June 24. The whole entourage had a birthday party, the highlight of which was a foot-high cake. When the festivities drew to an end, Jack took a breath and looked around. "Thus does all fun cease," he said. It was an odd statement from a man whose training camps for years had been marked by the maddest of fun.

For some years now, Dempsey had been guiding his own destiny, making the key decisions himself and simply leaving the money end of things to people such as Gene Normile. Now, however, Flynn took over—as a full-scale manager, not just the business manager he reportedly had been engaged as—and, somewhat surprisingly, Dempsey seemed to welcome the strict supervision. Flynn as much as told him whether or not he could have a second cup of coffee and Jack was almost meek about it.

Flynn bristled with confidence. "I can bring Dempsey into the ring to knock out Sharkey in four rounds," he said.

There was a brief argument among Dempsey, Flynn and Tom Luther, the owner of the camp, about an admission fee for spectators who wanted to watch Jack train. Dempsey didn't want any such fee, but Luther insisted on a dollar admission charge, to be split down the middle. It was estimated that enough curious people would come to the Saratoga Lake camp to bring in around $20,000 dollars. Dempsey finally gave in, saying, "Take my half and give it to a good charity."

Dempsey started his training slowly, but then picked up the pace. Sharkey turned twenty-four years old—eight less than Jack—on Monday, June 27. Two days later Flynn invited fifty physicians attending a New York State health conference in Saratoga to pick eight of their number to examine Dempsey. The medicos, as the sportswriters put it, found him in excellent health, but said he was at least three weeks' hard work away from being in the razor-sharp condition a boxer needed.

"I noticed an absence of that strained brain which he exhibited before the Tunney fight," one of the doctors said, as the sportswriters began toying with the words "strained brain" and wondering exactly what they meant.

In New York, Rickard said beamingly that, while tickets had not yet been printed for the fight, he already had $200,000 in advance orders in the till.

On Thursday, June 30, Dempsey worked four rounds with his sparmates on trying to evade left hooks and jabs —Sharkey's best punches—and the consensus was that he did passably. The reporters scratched their heads as they watched him engage in defending. In other Dempsey camps of other times, other years, the formula was routine: Jack would tear out of his corner, smash the sparring partner all over the ring and in general try to destroy him.

It wasn't in the cards for Jack to go along for even a few weeks without bad luck, however. On Friday, July 1, his brother John, who lived in Schenectady, killed his wife and himself. Dempsey made a quick trip to that upstate city, arranged for John's body to be returned to Salt Lake City, and returned to camp.

Flynn, who spoke in clichés, said solemnly, "It is a crushing load for Jack to have to carry," and there were strong rumors of postponing the Sharkey fight or even abandoning it entirely. Dawson of the *Times* called the tragedy critical to Dempsey because he was, in Dawson's opinion, "a long way from the Dempsey of old."

Dawson had a point. Although tanned and superficially trim, Dempsey still was a bit overweight, a trifle flabby across the back, and had a slight belly; and he knew it, too. The day before the Fourth of July, he and Flynn agreed that he should work in secret, and a thousand persons were turned away from the camp. Even the reporters were barred from the ring area. Four state troopers with Colt .45's at their sides and a couple of Tom Luther's husky men-of-all-work supervised the barring. Rumors persisted that unless Dempsey's condition improved sharply, he might ask a postponement.

On Monday, July 4, the eighth anniversary of the Dempsey-Willard fight at Toledo, 2500 more prospective spectators were turned away . . . but this time the newsmen and a few of Dempsey's friends were allowed to watch as he boxed seven rounds. It seemed almost unbelievable that Flynn spent much of the time schooling Jack in protecting against a left-hand lead and how to stand facing such a strategist, after all Dempsey's successful years in the ring. But Jack took it patiently and even seemed to enjoy having a drillmaster.

In New York, Sharkey still hadn't shown up to begin working out at the Garden roof, and Buckley told reporters rather lamely, "He just couldn't do it." Sharkey, however, was reported working out with some regularity in Kelly and Hayes' gymnasium in Boston.

Dempsey began to improve a little. He started ripping into his good sparmates and even knocked one out of the ring. James J. Corbett, the champion of another day, traveled up to Saratoga and was admiring. "I came up here expecting to look at an old broken-down warhorse," he said. "Instead, I looked at a good fighter. It will take a great fighter to beat him."

And Dempsey wired Rickard: FIRMLY CONVINCED I WILL BE FIT AND READY TWENTY-FIRST. POSITIVELY NO POSTPONEMENT. DON'T WORRY.

IN PARIS, Byrd and his crew were being given the banquet treatment, and at one of these fetes the commander predicted "great powerful planes, which will fly at great altitudes, say eighteen to twenty thousand feet, in fifteen years." Some of them, he said, would have six engines. And in the Hearst papers in America, Arthur Brisbane announced that Henry Ford had ordered his publication, the *Dearborn Independent,* to "discontinue permanently" articles hostile to Jews. Ford was quoted as saying he was "deeply mortified" that such pieces had been published, but in Detroit, editor William J. Cameron said he was somewhat surprised and couldn't believe that Ford would make such a statement without advising him.

SHARKEY FINALLY came into New York to start training at the Garden roof, accompanied by his wife and trainer Harry Kelly. Three hundred New Yorkers dropped by to see his first workout, a light one involving three rounds of sparring, and most onlookers thought he looked pretty good.

In Saratoga, Dempsey seemed to give conflicting impressions. Some days he sparred well and seemed cheerful. Others, he didn't look good at all and was disgusted. On Thursday, July 7, he went golfing with Flynn, middleweight Dave Shade, Jerry the Greek, Joe Benjamin and some writers. When his drive went into the rough on the ninth hole, he knocked off and went berry picking. The next day he knocked down two of his sparmates, but the writers still thought he looked slow.

Tex Rickard came by on Saturday and watched the "secret" workout, after which he said he was satisfied. Dempsey, he said, was "far different than last year in Atlantic City. On the outcome, of course, I must be neutral. I want both boys to win." Tom Luther, meanwhile, grumbled that barring the public already had cost him $12,000 and said he understood he was going to get a settlement of $10,000 from the Dempsey people.

Sharkey suddenly developed into a crowd puller. On

Sunday, July 10, he did some early roadwork, attended Mass at St. Malachy's Church in Manhattan, and then worked out before 1500 spectators at the Garden.

He was a pretty sight on the light bag, having worked up a little routine there, and when he got into the ring with sparring partners, he sometimes danced around with hands at his side after the fashion of the Fancy-Dan Irish boxers. He kept looking at the audience and winking at the fans.

Dempsey would work a day, then take off a day; he had three holidays in one week. His weight was still up there, at 205, and he talked vaguely about remaining in the East until after the Tunney bout. He said that after he beat Sharkey he would go to the Maine woods to rough it for a while before meeting Tunney, but the writers were beginning to doubt more and more that he would meet the champion.

Two thousand tourists, some of whom were in Saratoga for a Knights of Columbus outing, showed up on Sunday, July 10, at Dempsey's camp, and were disappointed when he didn't appear. Meanwhile, Leonard Sachs returned from New York with disappointing news for the camp entourage. Dempsey's followers had raised a pool of $5500 seeking to get down a six-to-one bet that Jack would win back the title—in other words, a two-bout parley—but the best odds Sachs could dig up were four to one.

On Monday, July 11, Dempsey's workout was opened to the public, and a band of socialites including Mrs. Raymond T. Baker and a party of friends turned up. The boxers Johnny Dundee and Benny Leonard also were on hand. Dempsey put on an enthusiastic, hard-hitting performance, boxing six rounds, but still didn't look too good. He was caught off balance frequently, was wilder than usual, and took quite a few punches himself. The writers decided he would have to knock out Sharkey to win, and one wrote that Jack was hampered by "lack of coordination between his mind and his hands and feet."

He could have written it shorter, of course: age.

Back in New York, the crowd of Sharkey fans swelled to 2000 as he put on another sparkling exhibition, knocking out one of his partners, Johnny Urban. Corbett was present for this workout; his guarded comment was that Sharkey looked in good shape. Rickard, meanwhile, said the ticket sales had passed the $650,000 mark.

In Paris, where he had shepherded Mickey Walker for a bout, Doc Kearns decided to get into the act once more. He and Walker would sail for America from Cherbourg on Wednesday, July 13, he said, and would be in New York July 20. "I want to collect the money due me," he said, "and if such collection interferes with the fight, then I am sorry."

ONE OF THE features of summertime in the Saratoga–Lake George area in those years was the annual marathon swim of twenty-eight miles in Lake George. When the 1927 event began on Tuesday, July 12, Dempsey came over to help start things and ended up as a minor hero.

Jack and some of his party had zoomed up the lake to Hague, New York, in a speedboat, and as they stepped onto a pier, a crowd of persons rushed forward to see the ex-champion. A twenty-foot portion of the dock gave way and plunged a couple of dozen of them into the cold water, which was about five feet deep. Dempsey waded to shore, grinning, but when he saw a young woman, Clarissa Harlowe of Boston, struggling in the water, he waded out and rescued her.

The party went back to Saratoga none the worse for wear, except for a bruised shin on Fred Tapscott, one of Dempsey's bodyguards. Jack took off his wet clothes and went to bed in mid-afternoon, while Flynn talked with the sportswriters, with whom he disagreed sharply about the way Dempsey had looked in training. "I wish the fight was tomorrow night," he said decisively, adding that they would break camp next week, drive to Albany and then take the night boat to New York City.

The ticket sale passed $750,000 and, in reaction, the value of Madison Square Garden stock on the open market increased $1,250,000. The stock—which traded as voting trust certificates on the curb market—totaled 322,560 shares. It had been 16; now it shot up to 21¾. But, of course, stocks were always going up everywhere, day by day, in the golden land.

On Wednesday, July 13, a heat wave settled over most of the East. The mercury reached ninety-one in New York, and seventeen deaths were reported along the East Coast. Heedless of the muggy, stifling weather, Dempsey went through a long drill, including seven rounds of sparring, and again he looked unimpressive. Larry Gaines, the quick-moving Toronto Negro, backpedaled and peppered Jack with left-hand leads, jabs and hooks. One hook drew blood, and the sportswriters watched silently, glumly, realizing that these were Sharkey's best tools.

A couple of hundred spectators had been allowed to pay their way in, but Flynn had flip-flopped again and said he would bar them in the future. "Dempsey can't do himself justice when they're here," he said, pointing out that before a crowd Jack simply went out and tried to knock out the sparmates, while when only newsmen were on hand he contented himself with working on defense and moves.

News of the poor workout reached the big cities, and Dempsey, previously a nine-to-five favorite, fell to six to five. It was estimated that $400,000 had already been bet in New York City alone.

Sharkey, who still didn't seem to have "cut loose" in his workouts, took the night off from his early-to-bed routine and went to Ebbets Field in Brooklyn to watch Paolino fight Wills. Eighteen thousand were on hand as the two fought sloppily, and the Basque knocked out the Negro in the fourth round. Sharkey watched almost scornfully, and after the verdict he looked over at Paolino and held up one finger, indicating he would knock out the squat heavyweight in either one round or with one punch.

The writers noted with interest the difference between the two camps. Flynn still was the martinet at Saratoga. He ordered Dempsey to cut out roadwork—"No one ever won a prizefight running up and down hills"—and also had Jack work out with Dave Shade in the early morning before the hung-over sportswriters were up. Dempsey obeyed almost meekly. In New York, meanwhile, whenever Buckley and his aides told Sharkey to work on some aspects of offense or defense, he did exactly the opposite.

If Sharkey could evade the Dempsey punch for, oh, six

rounds or so, he had a good chance to beat the Manassa Mauler, the writers decided.

ON FRIDAY, JULY 15, thousands of Communists staged a sudden revolt in Vienna, seeking a Soviet republic of Austria, and 250 were killed and more than 500 wounded before police and government troops got things under control. At the famous old St. Andrews golf course in Scotland, 20,000 spectators rushed in at the eighteenth green and hoisted Bobby Jones to their shoulders after he had retained his British Open crown—while at Saratoga Lake the sportswriters had their daily Flynn chuckle. Leo, it seemed, had wired the State Athletic Commission requesting that indelible lines be drawn around the waists of Sharkey and Dempsey to indicate the foul boundaries.

The camp was getting ready to close down now, and more and more of the sparmates were released and sent on their way. Dempsey continued working out lightly and even sparred a couple of rounds. He slugged it out with Tilly (Kid) Herman, a Mexican middleweight, and had the lighter man shaky but couldn't floor him.

At this point there wasn't too much the writers could dispatch to their papers that was new, so they did "think" pieces. Dawson mourned "what is left of the once-great fighting machine" that was Dempsey, and Alva Johnston wrote a comic piece about the writers having called four of the last five bouts wrongly and said that now "they are on their mettle."

Johnston dealt with Dempsey's finances, too. He hinted that Dempsey, who was already president of a coal-mining corporation and a director of a chain of

163

hotels, would soon shuck these duties, or, as he put it, "after September, a big financial institution will close its doors." Commenting on Tunney, he noted that Gene "already has the curiously glazed and tinted complexion found in presidents and chairmen of the board."

It seemed apparent that Dempsey would go into the ring the underdog for the first time since the Willard fight eight years before. A new set of odds to appear was three to one against Dempsey winning by a knockout. It was now estimated that $500,000 had been bet in New York City, and the press requests for free seats passed the 500 mark. Western Union reported that in the past two weeks forty-nine correspondents had sent out 255,781 words from the two training camps.

LOU FINK, TUNNEY's trainer, masseur and man of all work, dropped by Dempsey's camp on Sunday, July 17, and said that Gene had throttled down to light training. Flynn, meanwhile, sent out a hurry call for Burke, Shade, Herman and Gallagher to return to camp, feeling that idleness might have blunted Dempsey's fine edge. However, he declared he already had made a down payment on a site for Dempsey to train for the fight with Tunney in September.

The next day New York City was busy with a huge reception for both Byrd and Chamberlin and their crews, and it rained. In Saratoga, Dempsey's left arm was wrapped in bandages soaked in camphorated oil and Flynn said Jack had irritated it slightly while sparring. In Hollywood, California, Jim Jeffries, now a farmer in the San Fernando Valley, picked Sharkey to win. Rickard made a statement to the press to the effect that, in spite of

Dempsey's reported ailments and dubious condition, the bout would go on. And the writers who had been with Dempsey went down to New York to see Sharkey work out. Their collective comment was, "Is that the best he can do?"

On Tuesday, Dempsey had both arms bandaged, and Flynn said this had been done to keep them limber, as with a racehorse. The writers guffawed. The odds went up to two to one favoring Sharkey, probably because of the news of Dempsey's infected arm. Doc Kearns wired to a friend in New York: ARRIVE WEDNESDAY. WALKER READY TO SUBSTITUTE IF COURTS PREVENT DEMPSEY MEETING SHARKEY. The good doctor, of course, was overlooking no bets.

On Wednesday, July 20, Ferdinand, the Hohenzollern king of Rumania, died in Bucharest after a long illness. His grandson, Prince Mihail, was elevated to power, as Prince Carol went into exile in Paris by order of Premier Jon Bratiano. In New York City, Boxing Commissioner George F. Brower blew the whistle on his fellow commissioners, James A. Farley and the ancient Muldoon.

The *Times* carried a front-page story in which Brower accused the other two of having set the $27.50 top ticket price for the big fight, which, he claimed, was foolish and harmful. The commission, Brower continued, had "not a vestige" of authority to tell a promoter the price he should put on his goods. "If the price is fixed below that which the public is willing to pay," he said, "speculation is bound to result." Farley maintained a dignified silence in reply. Muldoon said, "We have the right," and went on to maintain that boxing would suffer in the eyes of the public if there was no ceiling and very steep prices were allowed. The commissioners let it rest there.

As his own commentary on this story, Rickard opened his books to the public and disclosed that the commissioners themselves had received $3465 worth of free tickets for the fight and had bought large numbers of additional tickets. Farley, he said, had bought 282 tickets worth $9024, Brower 136 worth $4532 and Muldoon 50 worth $1375. The total of free and bought tickets for the commissioners was 594; thus, $18,316 worth of pasteboards were taken off the market.

Rickard also revealed the list of block purchasers. Hayden, Stone and Company was the largest, having bought 500. Tunney bought 24, and a half-dozen were purchased by Franklin Delano Roosevelt.

It was about time for the writers to go and get some predictions.

From Dempsey: "Sharkey is no easy mark. It's either he or I, and I'm out to get him." From Sharkey: "You can take it from me, I am going in there to knock him out." From Flynn: "It won't go over six." From Buckley: "Sharkey by a knockout in ten." And down south in Buenos Aires, Luis Angel Firpo rubbed his cheek stubble thoughtfully and picked Dempsey to win.

The gloves to be used in the bout were custom-measured to the fighters' hands, made of wine-colored elk's skin (more pliable than horsehide) and stuffed with curled rabbit hair. Doc Kearns debarked from Europe and announced with a cheerful grin that he had no intention of stopping the fight. "If Dempsey is the real, fighting Dempsey," he added, "Sharkey has no chance."

In New York, Sharkey, finished with training, spent the day playing hearts with friends. Upstate, Dempsey got into Flynn's Rolls-Royce at Luther's camp and was driven to Albany just before noon to catch a train for the city. Just outside Albany they stopped at Wolfert's Roost Country Club and Dempsey held a putting match with Flynn, tapping in a sixty-footer on his first putt. Dempsey's party then went to New York City in a private drawing room, got off at 125th Street to avoid the crowd at Grand Central Station, and went to Flynn's apartment in the Grand Concourse, the Bronx.

Ten months of waiting, debating, worrying, thinking, training, scowling and sweating were over.

CHAPTER 12

This was Yankee Stadium, Thursday night, July 21. It was a good, soft summer evening and there were 72,283 persons present as paid spectators. "Perhaps you can imagine a swarm of bees many times magnified," Damon Runyon wrote, adding that all of Mr. Rickard's well-known millionaires were present.

"I made a hurried dash down an aisle," Runyon wrote, "and fell under the hurrying hoofs of fourteen kings of the world of finance, twenty-nine merchant princes, six bootleggers and five ticket speculators, all owners of estates on Long Island and of Rolls-Royce cars. Mr. Rickard moved about all abeam with pleasure over the gathering and chewing violently on a cigar."

Rickard had filled almost the entire baseball infield

168

with pine benches, and far into the darkness of the stands there were many binoculars and field glasses in use. The crowd started pouring into the big ballpark *en masse* about six o'clock, although the seats in the bleachers had been thrown open more than three hours before.

There were the customary wild rumors: The fight had been postponed. Dempsey had been killed in a car crash en route to the Stadium. And later there was to be one about Sharkey having died after the fight. These were routine.

The gate receipts totaled $1,083,529. Dempsey was to get $317,000 of this officially, although it was "reliably reported" that Rickard had made an under-the-table deal and Jack actually would receive $352,000, or 37.5 percent, instead of 27.5. At any rate, it was the third-largest purse of Dempsey's career. Rickard estimated that he personally had grossed $260,000.

Fans were sitting on billboard fences, subway trains, rooftops and the massive watertanks atop nearby apartment buildings when Dempsey entered the ring in a heavy white woolen sweater. The crowd roared, and it was apparent that from here on in, wherever Dempsey went, the "slacker" cries would be heard no more. Now the crowd wanted the old man to win.

As was the custom, prominent fighters were introduced before the main bout, including Tunney. Then Sharkey came into the ring in an old brown bathrobe and Dempsey got up and walked over to say hello to him.

The fight began.

It was evident almost immediately that Sharkey wasn't going to let Dempsey swarm all over him as he had swarmed all over Willard. Nor was Jack going to try. He went almost at once into a low crouch and began weaving and bobbing, but it didn't seem to bother Sharkey. The Bostonian, his cold blue eyes focused on the other man, moved quickly, from side to side, in and out, feinting, jabbing and hooking, and leading now and then with long lefts.

Sharkey began to edge into a long lead. He was landing a half-dozen punches to one for Dempsey, and some of them hurt the Manassa Mauler. But Dempsey had been hurt before. Scowling, trying, shuffling in toward Sharkey, he kept coming. He had, he said later, a plan in mind.

He couldn't have put it into words. What it amounted to, the plan, was out-gaming Sharkey. Outlasting him and being around at the end when the other called it quits.

In the second, Dempsey hooked well to the body with two lefts. He had dropped Fulton and Morris with punches like these, but Sharkey seemed not to notice. Indeed, in one of the early rounds, when he had Dempsey staggering a little, he paused and looked out at the crowd. "Here's your cheese champion!" he yelled. Dempsey, grim and desperate, kept soaking up the punches. As he said later, "He couldn't miss me with his left. He moved like a good middleweight. I thought he was going to knock me out."

In the fourth, Sharkey was a bit more cautious, but he still was the aggressor. He reopened an old cut over Dempsey's eye, a holdover from the Philadelphia fight with Tunney, near the end of the round. In the fifth, Sharkey shook up his rival with lefts and rights to the head, and Dempsey, still landing to the ribs now and then, held on.

In his corner, between rounds, Dempsey listened to Leo Flynn: "Keep boring in. Keep pounding 'em home until he folds up."

In the sixth, Dempsey slowly, laboriously, began to go after Sharkey. He was aching and tired, but he dug jolting blows home to the stomach. He thought he felt, or heard, Sharkey wincing. When he went back to his corner, Dempsey gasped to Flynn, "I think I got him now." He was bleeding nearly everywhere, from eyes, mouth and nose, but his eyes still were clear.

Jack O'Sullivan was the referee. Midway in the seventh round, he watched closely as Dempsey, now throwing more punches than ever, went after Sharkey. There was a flurry of inside punching and Sharkey turned to O'Sullivan and complained that he had been hit low. His complaint was nothing new. Sharkey already had beaten Bud Gorman, Jim Maloney and Harry Wills on fouls. O'Sullivan stepped in toward the two fighters and shouted, "Watch your punches, Jack. I mean you, Dempsey!"

A moment later, swinging almost wildly, Dempsey hit Sharkey first with a right-hand punch to the left leg—the *leg,* the left leg—and as Sharkey turned to get away from this latest charge, Dempsey smashed home a left-hand punch to the body. Where it landed depended on where you sat. Dawson of the *Times,* for instance, said he had seen Sharkey fouled four times with rights, but did not see the left hook to the body. Grantland Rice, W. O. McGeehan, Bill Corum, Runyon and Benny Leonard all said they saw a foul—but Jim Corbett, Paul Gallico, Tommy Loughran, Westbrook Pegler and Ed Sullivan, also at ringside, said there was no foul.

Clutching feebly at his lower stomach, Sharkey started

to turn to O'Sullivan. It was a mistake. As Dempsey said later, "What was I going to do—write him a letter?"

The Dempsey reflexes returned for a swift moment. Sharkey's hands were down—and Jack hit him with a short left hook to the jaw. The ex-sailor went down like a sack of wheat. O'Sullivan hesitated and started to bend over Sharkey. "You better get up, Jack," he shouted, "because I'm starting to count." Then he turned and picked up the count at four or five. At ten, Sharkey still was down, showing no inclination to get up. Dempsey, this time in a neutral corner, his face bloody and covered with sweat, held on to the upper strands of the ring to steady himself, and when he heard O'Sullivan count ten, he just shook his head a little.

There would be a fight with Tunney in September.

THE CROWD—its members included Byrd and Chamberlin (who had gone almost unrecognized), publisher Roy Howard, Franklin D. Roosevelt, Ziegfeld, Tom Mix, Madame Galli-Curci, Bernt Balchen and movie star Tom Meighan—stood in the summer night and watched Dempsey help Sharkey to his corner. Runyon wrote of the crowd: "I suppose you would call it a cosmopolitan assemblage. There were a lot of Chinese among the races represented."

Down at ringside a radio announcer tried unsuccessfully to get the Maharajah of Rutlam, a ranking Indian potentate, to comment on the bout. The newsmen followed the boxers into their dressing rooms, and the tired Dempsey smiled for them and said he certainly had felt Sharkey's punches but "never was in serious trouble."

Then he took off for the Belmont Hotel.

Dr. William H. Walker, the State Athletic Commission's official physician, visited Sharkey and gave him a cursory examination. He found "no surface indication of a foul" but admitted there could have been one. The Bostonian's handlers started making alibis to the reporters, pounding home the foul theme, but Sharkey turned to them brusquely and said, "Aw, shut up. It's all in the game."

Later he made an odd statement. "Where's Dempsey's punch?" he asked.

A decade later, however, Sharkey, sitting at a dinner table with the golfer Sam Snead, was to compare Dempsey with Joe Louis, both of whom he had fought: "I'll tell you, Sam. See that phone booth over there? Put them both in there and close the door and Dempsey would come out. He never stopped hitting you and didn't much care where or when. Louis had me down nine times and gave me the worst beating of my life, but he always stepped away and gave me a chance to pull myself together. Dempsey never gave you a chance."

Tunney, leaving with the rest of the crowd, gave his opinion that Dempsey's gameness had won the fight. Rickard stood around beaming, now and then feeling into his inside jacket pocket for a sheaf of paper. Teddy Hayes had attached $62,000 of Dempsey's purse for alleged back salary, but Tex had accepted service of the summons to keep Dempsey from knowing and fretting about it.

The writers sat back and started tapping out their stories on their portables at ringside. Dawson's story was one of melancholy. He called Dempsey "a shell of his former self" in a burst of originality, adding that "if Dempsey was poor, Sharkey was just a little better."

THE FUSS AND feathers weren't over so quickly.

The next day, July 22, the *Times* carried a huge front-page story on the controversial result, with Commissioner Farley quoted as saying that there would be no reversal of the knockout decision. "The commission never has reversed a decision of its officials," Farley said.

Dawson, evidently forgetting at least the Firpo-Dempsey bout if no others, wrote that "not in the history of boxing" had one fight caused so much discussion and argument, and he admitted finally that it had been a left hook that knocked out Sharkey.

Tex Rickard went to Flynn's apartment and conferred there with Dempsey. He said later he had reached an understanding with Dempsey that the Dempsey-Tunney return bout would be held in Chicago, in all probability, on September 15 or 22. Rickard also saw a private showing of the fight movies and said he was convinced there had been no foul. Johnny Buckley, however, at the same showing, said he was convinced there *had* been a foul.

After his talk with Rickard, Dempsey went out and played eighteen holes of golf, with three stitches in a cut over his right eye and another stitch under his left eye. He left at night for Wilmington to visit Mrs. Dempsey's parents once more, and said that he would proceed to the West Coast, rest three weeks and then come back for four weeks' hard training for Tunney.

Rickard also told newsmen that Dempsey had been "violently ill" on the train ride from Albany the afternoon of the fight, and thought it probably was due to some sandwiches he had eaten on the train. Flynn and others of the Dempsey group also were affected.

Throughout the city and country, the was-it-foul-or-fair controversy continued. Even Mayor Jimmy Walker got into the act; he said he hadn't seen a foul but it might have looked that way because Sharkey wore his boxing trunks quite high. Those who had listened to the match on the radio were a bit confused, since little or no mention had been made of any low blows. The National Broadcasting Company stated that announcer Graham McNamee "apparently did not see a foul blow," but noted, too, that "it is a strict rule of the boxing commission that the announcer make no editorial comment."

In Mexico City, *The Universal* devoted twenty-four columns to the event. Mexicans and Americans listening to the bout at the Hotel St. Regis and the American Club in Mexico had cheered Dempsey wildly. In Philadelphia a twenty-seven-year-old man died of injuries when, acting out the bout with a twenty-year-old friend, he was hit with a fatal left hook.

There were some absorbing bet payoffs. In Orange, New Jersey, haberdasher Nathan Weinberger, who had wagered on Sharkey, paraded for an hour around town in a tuxedo, high silk hat and white shoes, pushing a wheelbarrow full of bricks. In Gettysburg, Pennsylvania, undertaker J. J. Kerman handed over a coffin to Robert Strausbaugh of McSherrytown. And in Cape May, New Jersey, Horace Church wheeled 200-pound Simon Cohen forty-five miles to Millville in a wheelbarrow. (If Cohen had lost, he would have had to eat twenty huckleberry pies, which he hated.)

Tunney privately felt he had not seen anything at the bout to make him worry particularly over his September date. Publicly he said he had seen no foul. "To me," he said, "the punches were fair and I think I was in a position to see what happened in the ring." He added that Dempsey, to him, had looked better than at Philadelphia the year before.

"I can't underestimate him," he said, "and I don't intend to."

IN MASSACHUSETTS, Governor Fuller went to Charlestown State Prison and conferred with Sacco and Vanzetti, who were six days into a hunger strike. In London, 13,000 persons showed up at a farewell garden party at Buckingham Palace for the Prince of Wales, who was to leave shortly for a Canadian visit with Prime Minister Stanley Baldwin. The palace grounds were gaily decorated with a pavilion trimmed with crimson and yellow flowers, and the guests included President King of Liberia and King Fuad of Egypt. It was noted with alarm by social commentators that the Prince had packed only two uniforms in his luggage for the trip. In Boston 114 persons were injured and one killed as hundreds of thousands of people stampeded across the Common to welcome Charles A. Lindbergh. And in Mystic, South Dakota, President Coolidge permitted photos to be taken of himself panning for gold and trout fishing.

THE FUROR OVER the foul-or-no-foul episode died down, but slowly. On Saturday, July 23, the lost-and-found columns of the New York newspapers were filled with reports of mislaid items at the Stadium. Commissioner Muldoon said that henceforward broadcasts of boxing bouts would be checked "to protect children and people shocked at the mention of blood." The physical condition of a fighter, he said sonorously, was unimportant and entirely irrelevant to the progress of a bout, which was considerable news along Cauliflower Row.

Dempsey headed back to the coast from Wilmington and after acknowledging a wild welcome at the Atlanta railroad station, reportedly said that, win or lose, he would quit the ring after the Tunney fight. In his office at the Garden, Tex Rickard already was busy working on what he hoped would be his masterpiece, the September fight.

Tunney came down from Speculator with Billy Gibson and Billy McCabe, his old friend and adviser, and talked for two hours with Rickard, coming to agreement on most aspects of the planned match with Dempsey.

Rickard discussed for the first time the reasons why it wouldn't be held in New York. The Athletic Commission's insistence on a $27.50 top ticket price was one stumbling block, he said. Another was that he felt there wasn't an arena large enough in the New York area to hold the crowd for which he hoped. What he was thinking of, he added, was a bout in Chicago for a $50 top, although the previous top admission price for any contest in that city had been $10. There seemed to be more than just talk behind the idea of moving the fight to Chicago. George F. Getz, a Chicago coal millionaire, told reporters he thought the bout would be held there around September 15, with perhaps a $40 top. Getz added that he would be the nominal promoter, since Illinois law demanded that that spot be filled by a resident of the state.

Rickard's face was bright and dreamy as he reported that only two days after the Sharkey bout he had already received 2000 orders for Dempsey-Tunney tickets.

The crowds continued to cheer Dempsey on his homeward safari. On Sunday he was mobbed three separate times during a brief stopover and once just missed being cut by flying glass when a desperate fan pushed his hand through an auto window. He telephoned Estelle from New Orleans, and he also took time out to say there was "nothing to the talk" about his allegedly offering Doc Kearns $100,000 to drop his assorted lawsuits.

More aftermath. On Tuesday, July 26, Sharkey came out of St. Elizabeth's Hospital in Boston, where he had gone after a slight intestinal hemorrhage, and Dr. Martin H. Spellman at the hospital said it probably had been "due to the blows Sharkey received." The two judges for the fight, Thomas F. Flynn and Charles F. Mathison, filed a report by letter with the New York State Athletic Commission. Mathison said that "Dempsey struck Sharkey three times in the body, well below the belt," and Flynn added, "Two blows were a trifle low, but not enough to harm or disqualify."

The sportswriters, incidentally, wondered what fight *they* had seen after reading the judges' score by rounds. Dempsey would have won on a split decision up to the seventh round. O'Sullivan scored it Dempsey two, Sharkey one and three even. Mathison gave Dempsey three, Sharkey two and one even, and Flynn gave Sharkey four, Dempsey one and one even.

Dempsey continued westward. In Phoenix he told the

station-side crowd he would "nail Tunney the next time," and in El Paso he said bluntly that Sharkey's only fault was "he lacks courage." At Phoenix one of those in the crowd to shake hands with him was "Fireman Jim" Flynn—the only man ever to knock out Dempsey.

The rumors that Chicago would get the fight continued. Getz said everything was settled but minor details, and even Doc Kearns said he would shift his suits to that city. In New York, however, Jim Farley said it was his opinion that the Dempsey-Tunney meeting would be in New York (the state had collected a tax of $49,251.35 on the Dempsey-Sharkey fight), and there were reports that the commission would bend its laws and make a $50 top legal.

On Wednesday, the twenty-seventh, the "slacker" charge reared its ugly head again. A group of unidentified plaintiffs brought suit in Chicago to prevent the bout being here there because of Jack's war record, or lack of a war record. An attorney for the suers said his clients were American Legionnaires who were upset because Soldier's Field in Grant Park, the proposed site, had been dedicated to the doughboys of World War I.

Rickard just yawned and left for Chicago, with a roll of blueprints of Philadelphia's Sesquicentennial Stadium under his arm.

Dempsey had been cheered across the land. Now, as he arrived in Los Angeles, things became almost riotous. Fifty thousand persons shoved and jammed and crowded around him after his train pulled in, and three hundred policemen had to be called to keep the mob in check. Jack went briefly to a reception in his honor at a hotel, then rushed home to Estelle, who was slightly ill.

In Rome, *L'Osservatore Romano* said boxing was barbaric, in a blistering editorial. "This does not lead to ascension on the road to civilization," the editorial said, "but leads backward toward rapid ruin."

Rickard didn't seem troubled.

LATE IN JULY a squall blew across Lake Michigan and twenty-six excursionists were drowned. Eight of the bodies were recovered by Johnny Weissmuller, the Olympic swimming champion, and his brother Peter. It was reported that in the past eight years 137,017 persons had been killed by automobiles in the United States, or more than all the Americans slain in the First World War. And in Bucharest, friends of Marie of Rumania said the Queen, saddened by the death of Ferdinand, was contemplating entering a convent.

IN CHICAGO, Rickard went out to Soldier's Field and looked over the layout. "This is the only stadium in America capable of holding the crowd this match will draw," Tex said. "New York is pressing hard for the bout, but Chicago is the logical city." He then conferred with Getz for two hours. Meanwhile, Edward J. Kelly, president of the South Park Board of Chicago, said public opinion would determine whether the field should be used; he sounded out business leaders and invited the public to write its views to him.

"That war-record business is old stuff," Rickard snorted. "The war is a long time behind us."

The next day he told a meeting of Chicago businessmen he was confident that they had the bout, and, referring to Farley's opinion that it would be held in New

York, added, "Farley is all mixed up."

"Farley asked me, 'Tex, if you get this $27.50 for the Sharkey-Dempsey fight, will you promise not to ask more than that for the championship battle?' " Rickard said. "Now what was there in that that promised the fight to New York?" Back in New York, a disgruntled Farley said that if the bout were held in the Midwest, "it will be unfair and ungrateful of Rickard." He said that Tex had negotiated with the Chicago interests "without consulting" the New York commission about the possibility of a higher ticket charge.

Rickard was riding high. He received a letter from the Chicagoans who had brought up Dempsey's war record, and Tex said that "all opposition is now apparently thrust aside." He promised Chicagoans, "It'll be better than a national Republican convention for Chicago," and said the price range tentatively was pegged at $40 top and $5 bottom.

"I never in my life saw such interest in a fight as this here fight is drawing," he said.

As AUGUST BEGAN, the country gradually focused its attention on the imminent execution of Sacco and Vanzetti. The grim ritual was set for August 10, and six days before that date Governor Fuller said that he saw no reason for a new trial or for any executive intervention. Fifteen hundred persons rioted near New York's City Hall as police used clubs to quell them, and there was an ugly, angry mood evident in the United States.

Eighty miles east of Ambrose Lightship, near the entrance to New York City's waterways from the Atlantic Ocean, Clarence Chamberlin took off in a biplane from a

114-foot "flying bridge," or runway, constructed on the *Leviathan*, and navigated through a light rainstorm to Curtiss Field, completing the first known ship-to-shore flight. In Rapid City, South Dakota, President Coolidge issued a historic statement: "I do not choose to run for President in nineteen twenty-eight."

"Is there any other comment?" a reporter asked.

"None," Coolidge replied.

THE NEW YORK TIMES said on August 2 that the fight had been set definitely for Chicago on September 15, since Rickard had agreed to rent Soldier's Field for $100,000 and was quoted as saying, "It's all settled." Rickard left Chicago for New York the same day after having set back the date of the bout from September 15 to September 22 (Dempsey had asked for a delay to September 26). After the twenty-fifth, it seemed, Soldier's Field was booked solid.

Tex said that orders totaling $700,000 had been received already, and he expressed the hope that one fighter would train on the North Side of Chicago, where the Cubs were the baseball idols, and the other on the South Side, home of the White Sox. Back in New York, the Athletic Commission was still grumbling. Commissioner Muldoon disclosed that a letter had been sent to Rickard on June 30, saying that permission for the Dempsey-Sharkey fight at the Stadium had been granted "on condition that the big fight be held here."

In Speculator, Tunney at last began getting down to serious work. He ran four miles on the road early, did some bag punching and then went eight light rounds with sparring partners before quitting for some golf and fishing. Dempsey had other things than training on his mind, however. In Los Angeles his Estelle's condition was reported verging on the serious. She apparently was near a nervous collapse and seemed weakening, perhaps from worry over her grandmother's critical condition, and Jack wasn't thinking about boxing at all.

In Speculator, just two men were aware of something that happened that might have canceled not only the proposed fight, but Tunney's remaining boxing career.

Tunney had a few sparring partners on hand in those early days of slowly getting ready. One was a heavyweight named Frank Muskie, and as they were working out one day, their heads bumped. The top of Muskie's head jarred sickeningly against Tunney's skull near the temple. The men were involved in a punching duel at the time and almost immediately afterward Muskie hit Gene a long, hard right-hand on the jaw.

Tunney didn't black out—but he did lose all awareness of where he was and what he was doing. He went back at Muskie instinctively and knocked him out, but he still was badly shaken up and felt strange.

The champion boxed three more rounds, however, with Eddie Eagan, the collegiate champion, and that night went to bed early. It wasn't until the next morning, awakening in his cabin by the water's edge, that he really had any inkling of where he was. But he was a long way from better.

For three days he was in a slowly receding cloud. He had trouble remembering the names of even his most intimate acquaintances. He stayed in his cabin except to eat or go for walks, and he stopped training. He asked guarded questions, particularly so as not to alert any of the three newsmen assigned to cover the camp activity.

Gene told only Eagan about it, and it was only after some discussions they both realized he had suffered a concussion.

"The first seed of retirement was sown then," Tunney was to say later. "I felt as though hot water had been poured through a hole in my skull and had flowed down over the brain to my eyes, leaving a hot film. The possibility of becoming 'punch-drunk' haunted me for weeks."

CHAPTER 13

THE MOMENTUM was truly amazing.

By Wednesday, August 3, seven weeks before the fight, Rickard had a million dollars in advance orders in the till.

He rubbed his hands and announced solemnly that, wishing to avoid scandal, he would issue no complimentary tickets except for the press. A hundred and fifty thousand of his ornate gold-embossed tickets would be printed, and he studied plans to build up the open side of Soldier's Field on the north, to add another 35,000 seats. Rickard made the Congress Hotel, twenty minutes from the stadium, his headquarters and began shuttling back and forth between New York and the Midwest.

There was no mob-psychology expert around to explain the enormous interest in the return bout between the two men. Certainly Tunney had whipped Dempsey decisively in the first meeting. But then—thanks in part to the publicity following the first bout—there was a widespread feeling that the "real" Dempsey had not been on display that rain-soaked night. A blood-poisoned arm, legal worries, troubles at home, a three-year hiatus from fighting—a dozen reasons were advanced for Jack's showing in Philadelphia.

He had started to come back, hadn't he? He had knocked out Sharkey, hadn't he? The old Manassa Mauler would show them. Remember him at Toledo against Willard? Had there ever been such a fighter?

Estelle's health began to improve. Dempsey breathed easier and said he would leave for the Chicago area around the middle of the month.

Sharkey, who, it sometimes seemed, never stopped talking, said in Boston that he had an agreement with Rickard to take either man's place if necessary. For lagniappe, he threw in the opinion that Tunney could punch both hard and accurately, and also take a punch, and "will put Dempsey away by the knockout route."

Tunney seemed to be taking everything leisurely, almost lackadaisically. He sent for two good boxers, Billy Vidabeck and Harold Mays, to join his camp at Speculator, and early in August he took a day off to go over to Troy, New York, for an American Legion state convention. The regular wolf pack of sportswriters had not yet descended on the camp.

Rickard insured each fighter for $100,000. He also said he had heard from Dempsey that Jack would train for this one behind barred gates.

* * *

THE SACCO-VANZETTI affair was gaining as much momentum as the fight. To some it seemed incredible that the execution of a couple of simple Italian immigrants was arousing deep emotion all over the world, but there it was. Two thousand "radicals"—the description is a journalistic one—gathered in front of the American Embassy in Grosvenor Square in London and hooted for hours on end. In New York City, Sacco-Vanzetti sympathizers called for 500,000 workers to strike for a day and attend a mass meeting in Union Square, traditional home of left-wing causes, in downtown Manhattan.

They didn't get their 500,000, but 15,000 did show up and became involved only in minor skirmishes with the 400 policemen detailed to the square. In Rome, Sacco's father, Michele, sent a pathetic wire to Mussolini asking for his help, and Il Duce replied, "I have done everything compatible with international law."

The execution was set for 12:15 a.m. on Thursday, August 11. At 11:24 p.m. on the tenth, less than an hour before the legal slaying, Governor Fuller granted a twelve-day stay, to allow a State Supreme Court ruling on a writ of error.

The world greeted the reprieve with mixed feelings. In London 10,000 rioters led by a girl with bobbed hair were routed by police from in front of the American Embassy. *Time,* the news magazine, editorialized: "Society, through its legal machinery in Massachusetts, had started to bare the skins of prisoners Sacco, Vanzetti and Madeiros [another prisoner, who, condemned to death for one murder, had confessed in prison to having done the shooting in the South Braintree episode] for the touch of Death. Then, with a reprieve of which the melodrama was a cheap insult to whatever dignity human life may have, virtually mumbled *Live on for another twelve days longer. Our mind is not quite made up."*

RAGGLE-TAGGLE loose ends of the proposed big fight kept surfacing in public. Leo Flynn came by Rickard's Garden office and made the announcement that he would ask Illinois authorities to schedule the bout for fifteen rounds, although state law allowed only ten. (Apparently, however, Flynn never followed this up.) Billy Gibson began a tour of campsites in and around Chicago and said that, as at Speculator, no admission would be charged for Tunney's workouts. An application for a referee's license came from Oscar Matthew ("Battling") Nelson, the old lightweight titleholder; he wanted to officiate at the fight. "Everyone getting into the act" was not just a worn phrase.

Rickard, growing more optimistic by the hour, said now that 161,000 tickets would be printed.

Gibson found an ideal training camp, the Lincoln Fields racetrack near Crete, Illinois, thirty-five miles south of the city of Chicago on the Dixie Highway—but found that Dempsey had an option on it.

Tunney's manager visited sites at Antioch and Lake Villa, both forty miles northwest of the city, and was offered the Deering estate of seven hundred acres, fifty-one rooms, seventeen baths and so on. He finally picked the Cedar Crest Country Club at Fox Lake.

Flynn announced Dempsey's sparmates: Martin Burke, Dave Shade, Allentown Joe Gans, My Sullivan and Jack McAuliffe.

Rickard left for Chicago on Friday, August 12, in the company of Flynn and Gus Wilson, intending to stay there until after the fight.

Dempsey said he would leave Los Angeles on Monday, August 15, stop at Salt Lake City to see his mother and at Denver to see friends, and then come into Chicago.

Rickard looked ahead. He said he might hold a 1928 title fight in London, confident that 25,000 Americans would sail across the Atlantic to see it.

Ticket headquarters were set up in the arcade of the Palmer House in Chicago.

Back at the Stadium in New York, the hangers-on in the heavyweight picture kept at it. Jack Delaney, well ahead of Paolino on points before 30,000 fans, won on a foul from the Basque in the seventh round.

THE AVIATION whirligig was still in motion. On Sunday, August 14, the German monoplane *Bremen* took off from Dessau, Germany, on a flight to New York. Fog forced its sister plane, *Europa,* to return to home base after it reached the North Sea, and a day later the *Bremen,* too, had to turn back after twenty-two stormy hours in the air. In La Paz, Bolivia, 80,000 descendants of the Incas, armed with clubs and slingshots and chafing at what they felt had been suppression ever since the Spanish conquest, rioted and tried to burn down and rid their area of all vestiges of the white man. In Detroit, Henry Ford and his son took a short flight with Lindbergh and thus became the first and second passengers ever to ride in the *Spirit of St. Louis.* At the foot of Mont Blanc in the Alps, the secretary-general of the Italian Fascist Party rechristened the peak "Mount Benito Mussolini," although its base touched France, Italy and Switzerland.

In Shanghai there was word that General Chiang Kaishek had resigned as commander of the Nanking revolutionary armies, which had taken Nanking only to see their government collapse. And in Massachusetts, Sacco broke a thirty-day fast and had two mugs of hot beef tea, as the state's Supreme Court rejected all pleas to save them and the pair's defense counsel moved in the direction of the federal courts. A bomb wrecked the home of Lewis McHardy, twelve miles south of Boston. McHardy had been one of the good men and true who had convicted Sacco and Vanzetti.

WITH THE FIGHT FEVER building in Chicago, Dempsey came into town on Thursday, August 18.

A mob gathered at the Northwestern Railroad Station in the Loop, but Jack debarked from the Overland Limited at Oak Park, a suburb, and was driven to the Edgewater Beach Hotel on the North Side, where Estelle planned to stay. Dempsey was going to spend a few days at the Morrison.

Jack said he weighed 204 and wished he had even a little more beef "because it melts off in hard work." "I certainly will win," he said, almost perfunctorily, "and don't be surprised if I knock Mr. Tunney right through the ropes."

The money continued to pour in. On just one day, the previous Monday, $200,000 reportedly went into the till, although no more tickets were scheduled to be sold to the public until the following Monday, August 22. Rickard reported that a St. Louis civic organization had sent in a check for $35,000, presumably the largest ticket order for a boxing match in history.

Dempsey didn't go right to work. He spent several days at the Edgewater Beach with the convalescing Estelle, who was in the care of a Chicago specialist and two nurses. There was a spreading rumor that Mrs. Dempsey's condition was more serious than had been known, but Jack pooh-poohed it and reported that he had even taken her out motoring one afternoon.

Jack's growing popularity with America was astounding, especially in view of his past stormy relationship with the public. Marie Hannon, his secretary, and Leonard Sachs, his troubleshooting lawyer, said that he was receiving about 5000 letters a day from just plain fans, and another 1000 involving business propositions, as well as several hundred telegrams. On Sunday night, August 21, during a police track-and-field meet at Wrigley Field, Dempsey was made an honorary member of the Chicago Police Department, to the accompaniment of wild cheering.

At Speculator, Tunney stepped up his training program and by this time was really hard at work. The Right Crowd was still very much in evidence; one day, for instance, Harry Payne Whitney drove over from the races at Saratoga to see Gene work out.

ON THE MORNING of Monday, August 23, the city fathers of Boston shut down the Common to public orators for the first time in history.

All police leaves and vacations were canceled and the whole force went on twenty-four-hour duty, including riot squads, who were armed with tear-gas bombs, hand grenades and automatic rifles, and who went here and there breaking up ominous street-corner sessions.

It was a warm, clear summer day and Governor Fuller, entering his State House office, smiled at the mob of newsmen awaiting him. "It's a beautiful morning, isn't it, boys?" he asked.

All day long there was grumbling, shouting and city-wide discontent, and then, at last, night came. Charlestown Prison, where Sacco and Vanzetti were jailed and where they were to die in the electric chair, became an armed fort. A police barrier 1000 feet long was placed around the prison. Searchlights swept continuously across the yard and the walls, and machine guns could be seen jutting out along the parapets. Sacco's fourteen-year-old son and Vanzetti's sister Luigia—just in from Italy—visited the two men, but then the visiting time was over and midnight approached.

Only one newspaperman, an Associated Press employee, was allowed in the death chamber. As he told it, Sacco was the first to be strapped into the electric chair. As the straps were being fastened at 12:11 a.m., he raised a little in the chair and cried, *"Viva anarchia!"*

Vanzetti was brought in a minute after Sacco had been pronounced dead and removed from the room. Before coming to the death chamber, Vanzetti had made a statement: "I want to tell you that I am innocent and that I have never committed any crime, but sometimes some sin. I am innocent of all crime, not only this, but all. I am an innocent man. I wish to forgive some people for what they are now doing to me."

As he entered the grim room, Vanzetti went over and shook Warden William Hendry's hand, thanking the jailer warmly for his kindnesses during the long prison stretch. The warden was visibly shaken and looked as if he might faint. Then Vanzetti was strapped into the chair and the switch was pulled. He was pronounced dead at 12:26 a.m.

The jolts of current were felt around the world. There was great rioting in Paris, and in that city alone 200 persons were arrested. Forty thousand dollars' worth of damage—broken shopwindows and the like—was done in Geneva, and there were demonstrations in Germany, South America, Japan. According to *Time,* "The world scene was like a balloon full of illuminating gas with leaks which are invisible until ignited."

What some felt were Boston's long years of infamy had come to an end. But there was a residue. A few weeks before the execution, Phil Stong, a reporter for the North American Newspaper Alliance (and later author of the novel *State Fair*), had gone to the jail and talked with the two men at length.

Vanzetti gave him a statement that was made almost casually but was to be quoted for years to come (it was a focal point in the James Thurber-Elliott Nugent play, *The Male Animal*):

"If it had not been for this thing, I might have live out my life among scorning men. I might have died unmarked, unknown, a failure.

"Now we are not a failure. This is our career and our triumph. Never in our full life can we hope to do such work for tolerance, for justice, for man's understanding of man, as now we do by an accident.

"Our words, our lives, our pains—nothing! The taking of our lives—lives of a good shoemaker and a poor fish peddler—all!

"The moment that you think of belong to us—that last agony is our triumph!"

*   *   *

GUS WILSON AND Jerry the Greek spent several days out at the Lincoln Fields track, getting things organized and seeing that both an indoor ring and an outdoor ring were set up, the latter in front of the clubhouse. On Tuesday, August 23, Dempsey installed himself in residence, but he did no work. Cots for the sparring partners were put in the jockey quarters, and Flynn and Dempsey moved into Colonel Matt Winn's reasonably luxurious living quarters. He was the same Colonel Winn who was to become known as Mr. Kentucky Derby. Paul La Haye, a Canadian boxer who doubled as a chef, was brought in to cook for Dempsey just as he had in Saratoga, and Flynn made the announcement that, with the possible exception of a Sunday or two, the workouts would not be open to the public.

Dempsey was scheduled to start training the next day, but there was a rainstorm over the area and he decided to skip it. In Chicago, Mayor William Hale Thompson said with hearty generosity that he had surrendered his choice seats for the fight to J. Pierpont Morgan, who had cabled from London that he and a party of five would be in the Midwest for a meeting of the Pullman Company and would like to see the bout. It made an interesting story, but the J. P. Morgan Company calmly denied there was any truth in it. "Mr. Morgan never goes to fights," it was stated.

In Speculator, Tunney really began to cut loose. Sparring against Paul Cavalier, a very fast big man, Gene was swift and sharp and rarely missed a punch. A reporter asked him with a grin if he planned to fly to Chicago this time, for a little more psychological warfare, and Tunney said calmly, "This isn't important enough."

On Wednesday, August 24, Tunney varied his schedule by doing seven miles of roadwork and nothing else. In the afternoon he went out on Lake Pleasant in a rowboat with Johnny Hayes, the old-time marathon runner. Hayes rowed and Tunney read—although the older man kept trying to talk to him about the fight and the precautions that he, Tunney, should take. "You should wear a headguard to protect your looks while training," he said.

"I didn't have you bring me out here to tell me how good-looking I am," Tunney said. "Row on."

Still later in the day Dan Hanna, co-owner of the *Cleveland News,* came by the camp. He and several others picnicked with Tunney at Whiskey Brook. The whole camp seemed to be relaxing lazily. It was a bit different from the first days of training at the Dempsey layout.

At Dempsey's camp, Jerry the Greek, ever loyal, announced loudly that he was personally checking everything that Jack ate or drank, particularly the source of the water. Dempsey seemed almost somber. He denied the previous report that he would quit the ring if he won. He said that he would train to evade Tunney's left hand, but would not change his basic style and would keep "banging away until either I fall or the other fellow falls."

Tunney's camp may have seemed almost indolent, but Dempsey's was curiouser, to borrow from Alice.

Jack began "light sparring," as it was called, on Thursday, August 25, but promptly almost knocked out K. O. Christner, a good Midwestern heavyweight who had turned up in his training corps. On Saturday, Jack worked out seven rounds—and Leo Flynn, deftly changing his mind, allowed 500 of the populace to watch him. "We've decided to open the camp for the workouts," he said. Later Dempsey walked and trotted twice around the Lincoln Fields track.

The next day Estelle came by with her nurse and, from the top veranda of the clubhouse, watched her man going through his chores. Fifteen hundred persons were on hand this time. That night, after Estelle and they had gone, Dempsey put in a long session on a rowing machine, which he liked to use after dinner.

Fifteen hundred in Chicago; fifteen hundred in Speculator. But the New York contingent was disappointed. A light rain was falling and Gene found the boxing ring too slippery and dangerous, so he canceled the workout and went instead for a fourteen-mile hike. He said he would leave for Chicago on Thursday, September 1, on the Twentieth Century Limited.

Dempsey went golfing on Monday, again being elusive to newsmen, who were being kept from the fighter by a kind of elite home guard. It was a new experience for the reporters, who at previous Dempsey camps had spent long hours kidding and joking with Jack. On Tuesday 4000 Chicagoans showed up for his workout, including a number of notable local politicians, but Dempsey took off for the second day in a row. Flynn had another change of heart. The workouts would be open to the public only on weekends, he decided.

Finally Dempsey got back to work on Wednesday, August 31. Five thousand of the curious drove, rode the train, or walked to Lincoln Fields to see him. It was the largest crowd ever to watch him train for a bout, and Flynn picked up some small change by charging each car fifty cents for parking.

The crowd was a little dismayed. Dempsey appeared slow and, on the whole, unimpressive. He put in some good punching with Benny Krueger and Dutch Meisner, the latter normally a bricklayer, but against Jack McCann and Oak Till (a Rochester fighter who had sparred the previous year with Tunney) it was the same old story: Dempsey was hit by left-hands frequently. This had happened before the Sharkey fight, and now it was even more discouraging to Jack's fans. Tunney had a straight left that was even better than Sharkey's.

By contrast, Tunney, in his last workout at Speculator, was punching "wickedly hard" and boxing superbly. Never known as a knockout artist, Gene was a deceptive hitter. He landed "heavy" punches from his classic stance, just as, among equally fast baseball pitchers, some throw "heavy" and others "soft" fast balls. His sparmates missed punches against him at a ten-to-one ratio, and Tunney, perfecting an overhand right, punished them. The crowd on hand—including Jock Whitney, later our Ambassador to the Court of St. James's—was highly impressed.

The happiest man in the whole touring circus, however, was Tex Rickard. He reported that the advance sale had reached $1,600,000 and that he already had a million in the bank.

The unhappiest souls seemed to be the prospective purchasers of tickets. For one thing, Rickard had provided no seating diagrams to show them what kind of seats they might be buying. For another, they complained that Rickard's sellers were peddling some of the $40 seats for $45 and $50 because they were "extra choice," and that "specials" were going at three for $100 in the $30 section.

Urbanely, Rickard said there would *be* no seat diagrams. "A lot of people who would figure they were slighted," he said, "would make a wild dash to have their tickets changed. So you can see the situation that might arise." The public and the reporters spent quite a little time pondering that one.

TUNNEY LEFT upstate New York for Chicago on schedule the afternoon of Thursday, September 1, and for a little while there was some doubt he would make it at all.

It was raining heavily in Speculator when a parade of cars, led by the champion's and brought up in the rear by newsmen, started on the sixty-five-mile drive to the Utica train station. The rain didn't stop Tunney's driver from stepping on the gas. Once the auto skidded into a soft shoulder off the road and made a rut a foot deep. Coming into Utica, it skidded to within two feet of a stalled trolley car. Tunney took it all in stride, but the hung-over reporters were on the jittery side.

All along the road upstaters braved the rain to cheer him. At the Utica station several hundred crowded around Gene, including a band of a dozen small boys who took him over for ten minutes or so. Then, finally, he got onto the train and headed for what the sportswriters wrote solemnly was his date with destiny.

At his last meal at Bill Osborne's place in Speculator, his host had placed a cake with four candles on it in front of Tunney. "A four-round kayo," Osborne said, and Tunney smiled. "I'll try to oblige," he said.

* * *

198

BILLY GIBSON, already in Chicago, told the journalists that, win or lose, Tunney would make an around-the-world tour with Eddie Eagan after the bout. Gibson said that "several members of British royalty, now living in London," had influenced Gene's decision, and that he would hunt in Africa. Although John L. Sullivan had gone all over the United States and had traveled to Europe (one of his great admirers was the Prince of Wales, later Edward VII), as had Jim Jeffries and Dempsey, none of Tunney's predecessors had toured the world.

It was a long way from Greenwich Village.

Tunney arrived in Chicago a little before noon on Friday, September 2.

When Lindbergh had visited Chicago, he had received a tremendous ovation (he was on a three-month tour of the country)—but now, as the heavyweight champion of the world got off the Century at the LaSalle Street station, there was an almost equally hysterical turnout. Perched on the back of a touring car, waving and smiling at the crowd, Tunney rode through a storm of ticker tape in the financial district of the city, with a band marching noisily ahead. It was a hot midsummer day and perspiration was the order of the afternoon, but no one seemed to mind. Gene was driven to City Hall, where Alderman John Toman of the Twenty-third Ward, taking the temporarily absent Mayor Thompson's place, welcomed him in the council chamber.

"The talk," Gene said in a brief speech, "seems to be about some fight that is to be held, about which I know nothing. I am here to train for a boxing contest, not a fight. I don't like fighting. Never did. But I'm free to admit that I like boxing."

The crowd laughed and applauded loudly; at least the boy had a sense of humor. It didn't realize he was perfectly serious.

After the City Hall ritual Tunney and company headed first for the Congress Hotel for a brief visit with Rickard, and then to his training camp at the Cedar Crest Club on the shores of Lake Villa. The caravan moved swiftly, hitting sixty miles an hour, with a dozen motorcycle cops in the van. At one point one of the police cyclists hit a rough spot a hundred yards or so ahead of Tunney's car, and his machine spun around and crashed into two others. The policeman, Frank Truba of Libertyville, was injured seriously, and Tunney, leaping out of his auto, helped him to the roadside and knelt there with him until he was removed to a hospital. The caravan finished the trip more slowly.

RICKARD MARKED his twenty-first anniversary as a boxing promoter this day. It had been on Labor Day, September 2, 1906 in Goldfields, Nevada, that he presented the Nelson-Gans lightweight match.

He told reporters that he had fired two of his ticket sellers who had been offering the "de luxe specials" to the customers, but there was nothing he could do immediately about what seemed to be a rash of lawsuits that had trailed the fighters to Chicago.

First of all, one B. E. Clements, president of the Coliseum Athletic Club, filed a petition in Circuit Court for an injunction to halt the fight. Clements said he had bought the Wills-Dempsey fight contract from Floyd Fitzsimmons several years before. (He had actually obtained a restraining order for the first Dempsey-Tunney fight in 1926, but he had obtained it in Indiana, and the Pennsylvania courts refused to recognize the jurisdiction of another state's courts.)

Then there were Tim Mara, the New York sportsman, Jim Mullen, a Chicago promoter who had helped legalize boxing in Illinois, and Boo Boo Hoff, the Philadelphia hood. All were in the wings with suits, both Mara and Hoff claiming they had contracts guaranteeing them a percentage of Tunney's earnings.

Thousands still were turning out to see Dempsey work. The added income evidently turned Flynn momentarily from his plan of having public workouts only on weekends. Jack worked again on a defense against a left jab and Flynn seemed pleased. Newsmen who liked him were troubled, however. Watching him, they felt he needed work. Lots of work. Yet at this point Dempsey was still only working one day on and taking off the next. For example, he was scheduled to work out on Saturday, September 3; but when Will Rogers and Governor Len Small of Illinois made a trip out in hopes of seeing him spar on Friday the second, they had to settle for conversation.

It was three weeks till the big bout, and to the reporters—and even the broadcasters, for WLS had a broadcast team at ringside in Lincoln Fields, reporting over the wireless at 1:00 p.m. daily—the Manassa Mauler seemed to be going toward *his* date with destiny in odd fashion.

CHAPTER 14

I T W A S B E G I N N I N G to seem to some that the eyes of the universe were focused on Chicago, but in truth it wasn't quite that way. Jimmy Walker, for example, was traveling in elegant leisure around Europe—with Mrs. Walker, for a bit of a change. On the Lido, near Venice, he took a trolley ride alone in the early morning. "I am always studying transit problems everywhere I go," he said gravely.

Lita Grey Chaplin was $825,000 wealthier after her divorce settlement from Charlie. It was beginning to look as if Herbert Hoover, the Secretary of Commerce, would run against Al Smith in the 1928 Presidential election. Al Capone appeared to have hired a press agent, and the feds were getting ready to parole Earl Carroll because of good behavior. The book publishers were getting ready with their big books for the fall. It would be the autumn of Katharine Brush's *Little Sins,* Willa Cather's *Death Comes for the Archbishop,* Ernest Hemingway's *Men Without Women,* Mazo de la Roche's *Jalna* and P. G. Wodehouse's *Carry On, Jeeves.*

The movies were offering *Dracula, Underworld, The Big Parade, The Patent Leather Kid* and *Seventh Heaven.* The big news in films was, of course, Al Jolson's appearance in *The Jazz Singer,* in which a bit of dialogue and three songs by the razzmatazz Al were incorporated into the production. It was the first "talkie." Henry Ford had put ten million Model T's—the memorable tin-lizzies—on the road, but now he had shut down production and was getting ready to switch over to the manufacture of the Model A. The early Broadway shows were trying out, out of town—*The Trial of Mary Dugan* with Ann Harding, *Four Walls* with Muni Weisenfreund (soon to change his name to Paul Muni), *High Gear* with someone named Shirley Booth, and *Burlesque.*

It was business as usual. Frenetic, whoop-de-do business as usual.

TROUBLE STILL dogged Dempsey. On Saturday, September 3, working out with Benny Krueger before a crowd of 2500 that included Estelle, he went after Krueger eagerly, half-shoved him out of the ring, and then the two boxers tumbled to the ground, almost hitting a nearby brick path. Dempsey got up a little shakily, but went on with his workout, finishing the day with a cut lower lip. His partners continued to hit him with lefts.

Dempsey and Flynn both laughed at Tunney's City

Hall statement about coming to Chicago for a "boxing contest." "I guess Gene doesn't choose to fight in 1927," Flynn said. "Well, Dempsey came to fight."

The literate sportswriter Richards Vidmer took his first look at Tunney since the year before and said he found him much bigger, larger around the neck and across the shoulders. Billy McCabe, who had quit his job as confidential agent for the Inspector of Prisons in New York City to be with Gene, confirmed Vidmer's findings. Tunney, he said, *was* bigger and stronger, "but not nearly so good as he will be." Actually, like many Irishmen who continue to grow until well into adult life, Gene hadn't reached his full height until he was twenty-five.

Vidmer added that "perhaps Gene has added a few books to his library, a few six-syllable words to his vocabulary," but otherwise was unchanged personalitywise. He recalled that in 1926 Tunney had told him, "It's in the cards that I win. I've worked faithfully and earnestly to win the title and so I shall."

The crowds continued to flock to Lincoln Fields, feeling, perhaps, it might be one of their last looks at the now almost legendary Dempsey. Eight thousand men, women and children showed up on Sunday, September 4, for a "take" of $10,000, but suddenly Leo Flynn was upset again. The crowd, he said, was unruly and upset Jack. The crowd rushed to three sides of the exercising platform alongside the outdoor ring and, as Dempsey went eight slow, awkward rounds with his sparmates, taunted him about his missing punches. "I don't intend to have people in here the way they were today," Flynn shrilled.

Tunney spent that Sunday going to church and golfing, but the next day he started training at Cedar Crest.

He boxed six brief rounds before about 5000 fans, then put a towel around his shoulders and left. His audience wasn't as crude as Dempsey's, but it was loud and noisy and he frowned at it several times, which seemed to work as a silencer. Dempsey worked seven rounds and looked good before 3000 persons, and the only other news of the sunny, hot day was that Flynn was thrown from a saddle horse when a rein broke.

Tuesday was something of an off day. Tunney boxed a bit, but when Chuck Wiggins butted him and opened a cut over his left eye, he stopped work and also canceled the morrow's drill. The humidity seemed to be bothering him, after the freshness of the New York mountain climate.

There were no signs of life in the Dempsey camp. Jack had gone the night before to a huge labor meeting at Soldier's Field and, after having been cheered wildly, returned to the Edgewater Beach with Estelle for the night. He came to Lincoln Fields in the forenoon on Tuesday, napped for a while and then played a little golf.

Oddly enough, the entire activity surrounding the fight at this stage was more or less unofficial. New contracts, necessary for Illinois, had not yet been signed by the two boxers, and Rickard hadn't even signed one for the field. There seemed to be a momentary lull in ticket sales, perhaps because of the lack of seating diagrams. Some business companies reportedly were trying to exchange or return tickets, but no returns were allowed.

Actually, there *were* three diagrams extant—one in Rickard's possession, one in Getz's office and one at the State Athletic Commission. Rickard guarded his zealously; if a reporter came in while the diagram was lying around, Rickard's secretary picked it up swiftly and locked it in a safe.

On Wednesday, September 7, Tunney did only road-work and later spent some time reading Maugham's *Of Human Bondage*. Vidmer wondered what Gene "was really after." "He is not a pugilist at heart," he wrote, "but yet, he is not 'high-hat.' "

Dempsey, too, lazed away most of this day. He played cards and fooled around with his campmates in the morning—to Jack, fooling around consisted of manhandling them—and in the afternoon drove to Highland Park for some golf with Jerry the Greek and Flynn. Flynn drove seventy miles per hour for a while, but it wasn't fast enough for Dempsey, who took over the wheel of their roadster and soon lost the following newsmen.

If you were assessing Dempsey after his Thursday, September 9, workout, it depended on what angle you were surveying from. Both Flynn and the sportswriters thought Dempsey stopped too many left-hand punches —his lip was cut again—but Dr. Joseph L. Russell, the State Athletic Commission physician, checked Jack over and said, "I have never examined a more perfect specimen of an athlete."

At Tunney's camp, meanwhile, Sergeant Bill Smith of the Chicago police had a complaint or two. Smith was in charge of a cordon of city and state cops who were posted along the lakefront, at the camp entrance, near the main highway, and in the surrounding woods.

"I've followed stick-up men through LaSalle Street at the rush hour," the sergeant said. "I've shadowed thugs from one end of Michigan Boulevard to the other—and I never found a man yet who could lose me . . . until I got this job. I think Tunney's in his room and then he walks in the front door with a book under his arm."

Life was pleasant for Tex Rickard, meanwhile. He reported that 40,000 "ringside" seats were almost gone and, in a fit of daring, offered to bet a hat that the gate would reach $3,000,000.

BY THE WEEKEND the Tunney camp crackled with confidence. Lou Fink declared, "It's a cinch; Tunney can't lose," and he gave the opinion that Dempsey hadn't been as good against Sharkey as against Gene. Billy Vidabeck, the sparmate, said Tunney "will K.O. Dempsey for sure." And even Tunney himself said calmly, "Oh, I shall win, all right. I'm sure of that."

On Friday, Dempsey drove recklessly forty-two miles to a Chicago courthouse to appear for the Clements suit. On Sunday old Jim Jeffries appeared at his camp as, of all things, a fight correspondent. Twenty-seven Indians, Blackfeet from the Glacier National Park Reservation, showed up for a ceremony at which Dempsey was dubbed "Thunder Chief" by Chief Two-Gun White Cloud (whose head was on the buffalo nickel) and received a necklace of beads and eagle claws. After an early rain the skies cleared up and Jack worked out. Reporters spent the day wondering about Dave Shade. The fancy-boxing middleweight had been on the grounds for some time, but had not been sparring with Dempsey. The presence of nine arc lamps overhanging the outdoor ring indicated that possibly he was working out with Jack at night.

Shade continued as a kind of mystery character in the Dempsey camp when he turned up on Sunday, September 12, with a black eye. He said with a grin he had gotten it "falling off Flynn's horse," and Dempsey said no, no, Dave got it when he tried to settle an argument in a roadhouse. The reporters, however, decided Dempsey must be moonlighting with drills, and they theorized that not only Shade, but also Big Boy Peterson of New Orleans and Whitey Allen of Boston were being used as sparring fodder.

For the first time Tunney looked on the verge of going stale, perhaps because of the heat. Fighters always dread reaching their peak too soon before a bout and then slipping over onto the other side, mentally and physically. Rickard turned up for Gene's Sunday workout and brought Jim Jeffries with him. "He looked all right," Jeffries said simply.

ACCORDING TO a front-page story in *The New York Times* the next day, Tex Rickard said at the signing of the new contracts that Tunney was to be guaranteed a flat $1,000,000 for the fight, the largest sum ever paid to a boxer. Rickard also said that Dempsey would receive $450,000. The same day Jack got a further bonus when the Clements suit was tossed out of court.

For the first time, now, people came right out and talked freely about the reports that had begun circulating: that there would be a "fix."

One of the most prevalent rumors was that, in addition to his legitimate million dollars, Tunney would receive another million under the table for "taking a dive." This was more or less standard for rumor mongering regarding a big fight, and indeed, because of the whole raft of unsavory characters in the game, there is little doubt that there had been many a dive. Even at this time, long years after the puzzling Johnson-Willard match in Havana, fight buffs continued to believe Johnson had deliberately thrown away his title. The wry Johnson, always ready to milk a publicity story, remained mysterious about it all and left people guessing.

If it was expected that the serious Tunney would bridle at these stories, however, it was expected wrong. Gene and his whole camp laughed at the idea. "No one can be confident of the result of a fight or sure of how it will end," Tunney said, adding with a smile, "If I'm to lay down, I'll keep that million for myself. Nobody will cut into that."

Later he would say that "all this stuff about fixing a fight is hokum." He insisted that no hoods or agents of hoods approached him before the Chicago bout, but he did say that Sergeant Smith, his chief bodyguard, paid a visit to Al Capone and told the scarred one not to "go overboard" on Dempsey, because Tunney was in good shape and was going to make a fight of it. Capone listened impassively and then bet $45,000 on Dempsey.

Nor did Tunney seem bothered by the almost open antagonism that some of the big-name sportswriters showed toward him. He said he philosophically accepted the fact that "Damon Runyon disliked me intensely" and that Ring Lardner, too, had little use for him. Tunney had some on his side, however: W. O. McGeehan, for example, a really close friend with whom Gene went hunting and fishing, and Grantland Rice. "It's just I didn't care for what you might call the rougher and readier ones," Tunney said.

Richards Vidmer, meanwhile, paid another visit to

Lincoln Fields and came away even more depressed. He said he had found Dempsey more closely guarded than ever, whereas in the old days Jack "let the world go by on its natural course and left an atmosphere of the unconquerable in his wake." Dempsey, he added, used to laugh at pessimistically written newspaper stories about him; now he read them all and seemed to worry over them.

BIG HEAT REALLY settled in over the Midwest. On Tuesday, September 13, the mercury reached ninety-five and there was no relief in sight at all. Both boxers called off their workouts, Tunney going to Lake Forest thirty-three miles away and staying with friends, and Dempsey going out to the races at Washington Park. He had, he noted, decided to abandon golf from now on during training because he concentrated and strained too hard on each shot and it took too much out of him.

Ticket sales rolled along. Getz filed a $1,000,000 insurance policy to protect the lessors of Soldier's Field, and in New York City two men were arrested for counterfeiting tickets. A few leaks about the seating plan trickled out, and it was discovered that the fans in the $5 seats, at the north end of the stadium, would be more than 700 feet from the ring. The ring itself, a 16-foot affair—seemingly to Dempsey's benefit, since Fancy Dan boxers usually try to get 20-foot rings in which they can maneuver more—was to be set on the 35-yard football line. There were to be four rows of actual working-press seats around the ring, and the telegraphers were to work beneath the canvas itself.

The report of the great distance between some of the seats and the ring got wide circulation, and Rickard found the sale of the cheaper tickets lagging considerably. He professed not to understand it. "In New York," he complained, "the town walks all over itself trying to buy the cheaper seats."

The legal picture brightened still further for Dempsey when Mullen abandoned his court plans. Tunney, too, got a break when Boo Boo Hoff said he would postpone his suit for a cut of Gene's earnings until after the fight.

On Wednesday, September 14, it still was almost unbearably hot and Dempsey went again to the races, with Leo Flynn and others. There, pressured by a reporter, Jack admitted finally that he *had* been working out at night, having boxed seven rounds secretly Tuesday evening.

"Jack is self-conscious before crowds," Flynn said sagely, adding that he and Jack were working on "some changes" in Dempsey's style of fighting, which to the newsmen seemed highly improbable.

A rainstorm on Thursday, September 16, cooled off Chicago, and both Gene and Jack went back to working out. For a change, Dempsey looked good. He was hitting savagely and wasn't being hit so often. He even outboxed the skillful Shade for a period and then knocked out Whitey Allen. Things were brighter around the camp.

By Friday, although he went ahead with his regular training schedule, Tunney had a red and swollen right eye. A specialist looked at it and warned that he had to be careful of complications. Jack Sharkey popped up at Cedar Crest, looked over Tunney as he boxed, and, in an uncharacteristic bit of humility, admitted finally that Gene looked good. As a rule, Sharkey worked on the theory that there was but one fighter and his name was Sharkey.

Dempsey continued looking even better, even when the heat and humidity returned. After his workout he spent a good part of the afternoon listening to grand opera on the victrola. He said he couldn't play any instrument himself but "the rest of the family all play something."

In the courts a new face appeared in the *dramatis personae*. The Reverend Elmer Williams, law-enforcement director of the Better Government Association and a well-known Chicago reformer, filed suit in United States District Court asking that the fight not go on. He said that Illinois law forbade charging more than a twenty-five-cent admission price to such goings-on. The bout, he said darkly, "will cast a cloud" on the war memorial that was Soldier's Field, but Charles S. Wharton, his attorney, glumly expressed doubt that the suit would even be heard before fight time.

THAT WEEKEND, September 17 and 18, King Boris of Bulgaria was in London, insisting that he had not come to England to find himself a bride. Packard announced twenty-eight new models of its famous cars, pointing out that "one of Europe's proudest reigning families" had just bought seven Packard straight-eights to replace the French cars it formerly used.

John David, the men's-wear store chain, was selling the best Irish poplin shirts for $2.75, and Douglas shoes were going for $5, $6 and $7. Listerine toothpaste cost 18 cents, and the James Butler grocery stores were selling coffee for 29 cents a pound and potatoes five pounds for 15 cents. The General Electric people proudly reported the advent of gorgeous new refrigerators featuring "ice quickly frozen in shining cubes."

On the green slopes of Mount Valerien in France, with Paris far below, half-hidden in mist and rain, 500 American Legion leaders stood at attention, along with General Pershing and Marshals Foch and Pétain, at a solemn ceremony of remembrance at the American cemetery in Suresnes. The 1500 white crosses stretching before the aging doughboys made a symmetrical and artistically pleasing picture.

TUNNEY RAN EIGHT miles on Saturday morning, but his eye still was bloodshot and he decided not to do any boxing. In the afternoon he went to the adjacent estate of Otto Lehmann, a retired Chicago merchant. The old businessman wheeled out his ninety-year-old horse-drawn coach for Gene; it once had been the property of a Vanderbilt and before that had been driven from Brighton to London in record time.

Dempsey called off both his workouts, daytime and evening, and spent the day restlessly. There were rumors of dissension in the camp, but he paid no attention to them. He did some roadwork, had a rubdown and then lay down for a few hours. When he got up, he put on his ring trunks and punched the bag for ten minutes. He didn't seem to know what he wanted to do. He picked up a magazine, read the opening paragraphs of an article and then tossed it away. He sat in for a few hands of a card game but couldn't concentrate, and finally he took a brassie and a handful of golf balls and went over to the infield of the track and whaled away at the balls.

Reporters watched all this and agreed that, mentally, at least, Jack was coming up to the fight the right way. It was almost *de rigueur* that a boxer get edgy before an important fight. Whether Dempsey's physical condition was up to his mental remained to be seen.

THERE WERE by this time from 400 to 500 journalistic boxing "experts" in the Chicago area, and now they began filing their "think pieces," dealing with their own views and opinions.

Although Flynn had already said that Jack would wait this time for Tunney to do the leading, most of the writers thought this sounded ominous. Nothing in boxing can be quite so horrendous as two counter-punchers waiting for each other to press the attack. Most of the experts seemed to feel, in spite of Flynn, that Dempsey would "carry" the fight to Tunney.

A poll was taken of 122 other star athletes; 70 picked Dempsey to win, 50 were for Tunney, and 2 suggested a draw. Babe Ruth and Lou Gehrig, for example, both picked Jack to win, but Bill Tilden, Harry Wills and Benny Leonard all plumped for Tunney. Arnold Rothstein got into the poll, presumably as a "sportsman," and said, "Tunney is a cinch. I bet on him last year and will bet on him this time."

The writers decided it was time to sound out the principals. Tunney told them: "I feel confident of beating Dempsey and may even knock him out." Billy Gibson echoed this: "I don't think Dempsey will last five or six rounds."

Dempsey seemed, just a little, to be talking to himself as he said, "I'm going to win cleanly and decisively. I'm

214

going to show them that I've come back, not just part-way, but all the way." And Leo Flynn insisted doggedly, "He can beat Tunney. Tunney never was a real champion."

The matter of a referee came up. The names in the hopper were Walter Eckersall, once the All-American collegiate football quarterback and now a boxing writer for the *Chicago Tribune;* old-time boxer Joe Choynski; amateur sportsman George Lytton; and the professional referees Dave Miller and Dave Barry. As usual, however, there were no official indications as to which one would be the third man in the ring.

CHAPTER 15

For LONG YEARS Tunney had been a Dempsey fan. From the time the former champion had spoken to him so pleasantly on a Hudson River ferryboat, through the years when Jack was beating all comers and Gene was working his way up, he always had liked Dempsey's directness and candor and had admired greatly the other's fighting—and boxing—ability.

The two men were almost totally unlike, yet Tunney made no bones about his respect and liking for Dempsey.

On Monday, September 19, that respect disappeared. It was replaced by something close to hate.

Spread across page one of the Chicago *Herald-Examiner* was a long story about the two men—the feature of which was a letter, published over Dempsey's signature, in which Jack made oblique charges that Gene, through Boo Boo Hoff and Abe Attell, had tried to fix the Phila-

216

delphia fight in 1926 by "getting to" the referee and one of the judges.

It wasn't just any old slack-news-day story, something dreamed up by a fretful reporter. At his camp in Lincoln Fields, Dempsey said he had read the letter, approved it and, in fact, had sent it himself to a news syndicate.

In the article Dempsey was quoted as admitting that Tunney "gave me the worst beating ever," but said that before he got to Philadelphia he had been tipped off that "there's something phony about this fight. . . . Somebody with some sort of political power" in the Pennsylvania city was involved, he went on.

"I was to lose the decision," Dempsey wrote to Tunney (it was in the form of an open letter to the champion) "and if I hit you at any point lower than the top of your head and dropped you, that somebody would yell 'foul!' in your behalf."

Dempsey bluntly asked Tunney about "secret conferences" with Abe Attell, followed by Attell seeing Hoff "in behalf of you both." Jack also claimed that after Billy Gibson had a conference with Attell on the eve of the bout, the gamblers' talk was "Sink the ship on Tunney. He can't lose."

Attell, Dempsey charged, had been at Tunney's camp in Stroudsburg and, after a lengthy conference with Gene, had rushed back to Philadelphia "with your pure and innocent manager, Billy Gibson." Then, Jack went on, Attell went to see Hoff. "Whatever Boo Boo wants —well, that's what Boo Boo gets," the Dempsey letter said. Attell, he said flatly, was "a tool for the gambling cliques.

"Since then," he continued, "it is learned that some sort of written contract was entered into, involving Hoff,

Gibson and yourself."

Dempsey said he was puzzled by a reported agreement between Gibson and Hoff. The manager, needing money, borrowed $20,000 from the racketeer, Jack charged. Gibson agreed to pay back the loan with no interest if Gene lost. If Gene won, Dempsey said, Gibson was to pay back the money "and as a sort of bonus, give Hoff twenty percent of all your earnings as champion.

"You signed as a party to the agreement," Dempsey wrote. "Can't we all have a little explanation about this?"

Dempsey threw in another, unrelated charge. He said that "Bow-tie Jimmy" Bronson, one of Tunney's seconds, was the one who had inspired the original draft-dodger hue and cry about Dempsey, "picking me out of twenty million American men who were exempt from war duty." Bronson, Dempsey said, was handling Sergeant Bob Martin at the time and "wanted to toss me into the discard" and get the Carpentier match for Martin.

The cynics, of course, decided that Rickard, possibly a little disturbed at the slackening of ticket sales, had spurred Dempsey's move. But the move demanded some kind of reply and it got a couple of low-key ones.

Bronson contented himself, for instance, with saying that Jack had "stooped pretty low" and that it was a "pretty late date to prove he was back in the shipyards during the war."

To newsmen Tunney grimly said that if there had been any contract between Hoff and Gibson, it was invalid. And to Dempsey, his onetime idol, he addressed this:

"My reaction to it [Dempsey's letter] is to ignore it and its evident trash completely. However, I cannot resist saying that I consider it a cheap appeal for public sympathy.

"Do you think this is sportsmanlike?"

Billy Gibson answered the charge in characteristic fashion—by sliding around to another point. He brought up the fact that Flynn had wanted to have indelible belt lines painted on Dempsey and Sharkey, to make the latter "afraid the public would think he was dogging it." No one was quite sure what this had to do with the alleged Gibson-Hoff contract or Dempsey's charges.

Four thousand persons jammed Tunney's training camp that day, and Gene, told earlier of the Dempsey letter before he went to Mass, looked good in his sparring. He refused to wear headgear to protect his healing eye, and in his final round of sparring he was hit on the eye by Vidabeck, who also bruised the bridge of his nose. Gene was boxing and hitting as sharply as ever, landing right crosses over the left leads of Vidabeck and Jack Williams.

Later in the day Tunney played a little golf with Anton J. Cermak and Hype Igoe at the Chain-o-Lakes Club. In the evening he was served with a subpoena in the Reverend Williams' suit.

At Lincoln Fields, Dempsey said simply he stood pat on his charges, then went out and worked five fast rounds. He knocked down Rocky Russell with a hard right-hand and only Shade gave him any kind of trouble. Estelle, on hand for the weekend, said she wouldn't go to the fight or listen to it, but, rather, "just sit back and wait for the final report."

ON MONDAY, the nineteenth, Dempsey studied Tunney's return open letter to him and then looked up. "Does he think it was sportsmanlike," he asked, "when he agreed to that deal with Hoff in Philadelphia?"

219

There was a report that Jack had prepared a second open letter to Gene, saying that Tunney's reply had been "unsatisfactory," but Dempsey had no comment on this. Tunney, in the meantime, was merely sarcastic about the whole business, although to some it seemed that it really had gotten under his skin.

"They're breaking my heart," he said. "The letter has upset me so that I am afraid I shall not be able to go on with my training. Isn't it terrible?" He went on to say that "the Dempsey crowd is cooking up something. Lots of ugly rumors are floating around Chicago about this fight and what Dempsey has up his sleeve."

Rickard, meanwhile, was so holy about the matter that sportswriters had trouble keeping straight faces. "This stuff makes me sick!" he exclaimed. "What's the matter with Dempsey, anyway? If I was his manager, I wouldn't let him get away with this."

One newsman asked him if he didn't think the verbal battle between the two fighters would harm the sale of tickets, and then, as the *Times* put it, "Rickard preserved a magnificent silence and looked the other way." A bit later, he said $2,250,000 worth of tickets had been sold.

Dramatic as Dempsey's charges were, they really were not that new to Tunney. Before the Philadelphia fight, rumors and scandal reports had been almost commonplace. Indeed, Tunney had had a difficult time convincing Grantland Rice that there wasn't some truth to the report that Dempsey might have purposely lost the Philadelphia match to (a) win a bet and (b) set up a lucrative return bout.

"But, Grant," Tunney said to him, "do you think I wouldn't know whether Dempsey was trying? There is one fellow that a fighter can't deceive about the honesty of his efforts and that is his opponent.

"I tell you, there is no sum that could have bought the championship from Dempsey." And he also told Rice that before the contest Billy Gibson had made an offer to Dempsey: he, Dempsey, could have both ends of the purse, meaning an extra $200,000 or so in his pocket, if Tunney won. Gibson wasn't offering a bribe. He just made the offer so Tunney would get the chance at the title rather than Harry Wills, who was still technically in the running for the championship bout.

"But Jack evidently did not think I had sufficient chance of winning to justify his bothering with our offer," Tunney said.

Nevertheless, in the first contract for the Chicago fight, which was superseded by a second drawn up later, Gene insisted that these clauses be inserted:

"The parties hereto in the performance of their obligations hereunder will use all reasonable efforts to have the contest conducted with utmost fairness and to discover and expose to the other any circumstances, facts, or transactions involving any persons whatsoever which might interfere with the fairness of such contest and the management and decision thereof, and upon such information being conveyed from one to the other as required hereunder, the parties mutually agree to take such steps as are in their power to preserve the fairness of said contest in every particular.

"The parties agree to use their best efforts, subject to the consent of the State Athletic Commission of the State of Illinois, to provide that taping and bandaging of the hands will be done in similar manner as was done in the contest in Philadelphia between said Tunney and William Harrison Dempsey, that the kind and quantity of tape used on each of the contestants' hands and the type of bandage used will be the same for each contestant, and that the contestants will apply said tape and bandage in the ring before said contestant, and the Club agrees to use its best effort to insert this provision in any contract which it may make with Tunney's opponent for said contest."

CHARGES OR NO CHARGES, there was no doubt that the championship battle had caught on.

An estimated 14,000 hotel and boardinghouse rooms in downtown Chicago all had been reserved as long as two weeks before. Of the estimated 16,000 rooms on the city's outskirts, more than half already were taken. Room prices remained about as usual, but there was a new stipulation: the guest had to sign up for three days . . . or, in some hotels, five days.

Some staggering statistics were beginning to come to light. The passenger-traffic managers of the New York Central and Michigan Central railroads said they expected about 22,000 persons to entrain for the fight, and that already "specials" had been lined up from Newark, Rochester, Cleveland, Columbus, Cincinnati, Detroit, Boston, Toledo and Louisville.

The $30 and $40 seats were gone. If you wanted one, your only hope was to unearth an accommodating speculator.

Gambling impresarios estimated that by fight time $10,000,000 would have been wagered on the bout, $2,000,000 of it in New York City alone. Jack Doyle, a "betting commissioner," or high-class bookie, whose odds-making generally was accepted as logical, quoted these prices:

Dempsey: 15 to 1 against a one-round knockout, 8 to 1 against a four-round knockout, 2 to 1 against a nine-round knockout and 7 to 5 against final victory.

Tunney: 20 to 1 against a one-round knockout, 8 to 1 against a four-round knockout, even money against a nine-round knockout, 5 to 7 against final victory. In brief, you had to bet 7 to win 5, if you liked Tunney to win. Gene thus was a slight favorite.

The Chicago police department announced that all vacations and leaves had been revoked and that 2800 uniformed men and detectives, augmented by a squad of New York City detectives and police from nearby towns and villages, would be on duty in and around Soldier's Field the night of the fight.

It was reported further that no cushions for the hard board seats would be sold, since Illinois law classified them as dangerous weapons—although a pop-bottle concession was awarded.

Rickard gave out the line-up of his huge staff of employees for the bout: 2000 ushers, 400 ticket takers, 400 ticket inspectors, 400 "directing" ushers, 150 captain ushers, a 150-man fire brigade, 135 men in the lost-and-found department and, courtesy of the police, 10 patrolmen each to escort Dempsey and Tunney to and from the ring.

On Monday, September 19, Dempsey went for his customary roadwork in the morning, did some wind sprints over the racetrack, had a rubdown from Jerry the Greek and finally, just before noon, met and shook hands with 250 Harvey, Illinois, schoolboys. "Whatever you do," he counseled the boys, "lead a clean, honest life. Avoid the use of liquor and tobacco. That's the best advice I can give anyone."

There was an atmosphere of noisy cheer in the Dempsey camp. Gus Wilson was swaggering and predicting victory loudly. Jerry the Greek was arguing with anyone who cared to. Dave Shade was whistling happily, and Leo Flynn went here and there, the picture of total confidence.

Tunney, in his next-to-last workout, looked as good as he had all along. Vidabeck hit him low with a right-hand in one sparring round, but in the dressing room later Gene said it hadn't bothered him. To the onlookers, who included Benny Leonard and the old heavyweight Tom Sharkey, Tunney said serenely, "I am fit. I can honestly say I never felt better in my life."

ON TUESDAY, September 20, the two men tapered off in their final workouts of any consequence.

Tunney punched the bag five rounds' worth and ran five miles and that was it. His eye seemed completely healed. The mercury had plunged suddenly and unexpectedly in the Chicago area, and it was only a bit above forty degrees when Tunney, in lightweight full-length long johns, trousers and a buttoned-up wool sweater, did his roadwork.

Tunney worked casually on some new punch combinations, as Lou Fink held the heavy bag, and when he was finished he stepped on the scale. He weighed 189.

Tunney told the sportswriters that he would go into the city early Thursday morning and take up quarters at the

Hotel Sherman, to which he planned to return after the match. There was only slight mention of Dempsey as he talked with the reporters, and Gene gave the impression at luncheon with them that his great respect for Jack had been replaced by contempt.

While eating, he idly picked up a pen, dipped it into an inkwell and wrote something on a menu card. A telephone call took him away from the table and one of the writers picked up the card. "This weather won't help the contender," it said.

It seemed strange, very strange, to see Jack Dempsey referred to as the contender.

Dempsey also did five miles of roadwork, and in the afternoon he shadowboxed two rounds and punched the bag for three or four minutes. Most of his sparmates were gone as Jack, tense and eager, slugged away viciously at the heavy bag. In mid-afternoon old Hyrum Dempsey turned up and Jack seemed delighted to see him. He went into his quarters with his father and they stayed there together until dinnertime. One report had it that he had told Hyrum he would defeat Tunney inside of eight rounds.

There was action in the courts. Leo Flynn went to Chicago and heard Federal Judge George A. Carpenter dismiss the Reverend Williams' petition to have the bout stopped as "vulgar and brutal." The judge said that since 150,000 or so persons were expected to attend, the whole affair hardly seemed against the public benefit.

Judge Harry Fisher, meanwhile, took up the Clements suit. Dempsey was asked to post a $100,000 bond by Wednesday, to postpone the hearing, or risk the possibility of an injunction. Arthur F. Driscoll, Dempsey's attorney, said he would discuss the matter with Jack.

Jack Doyle reported in New York that the odds had declined from 7 to 5 favoring Tunney, to even money, and $250,000 was estimated to have been bet in that city on Monday alone. Packey McFarland, a well-known former lightweight boxer, bet $5000 at 6 to 5 on Tunney. And from the Illinois State Athletic Commission came word that there had been a switch in the ring size. It would be 20 feet square, not 16, seemingly giving Tunney, the boxer, the edge.

IN MIDWEEK fifteen planes started westward in a New York-to-Spokane air derby and two flyers in it were killed shortly after take-off when their aircraft crashed into a Long Valley, New Jersey, mountainside. C. W. ("Speed") Helman of St. Paul won the race, flying 2340 miles in nineteen hours, forty-two minutes and fifty-two seconds before gliding across the hills on the east side of Spokane Valley into Felts Field.

In New York, ground was broken for the world's largest suspension span, a $60,000,000 structure across the Hudson River from Fort Lee, New Jersey, to Washington Park on the Manhattan side. Several hundred miles off the Newfoundland coast, parts of the plane *Old Glory,* which had been trying to cross the Atlantic, were found in the water. Jimmy Walker and his party headed for Le Havre from Paris to board the *Ile de France* for home after his long safari through Europe.

TO THE LAYMAN the referee of a prizefight may seem a necessary evil who gets in the fans' way and who lets an infighter grab and hold too much, or not enough, de-

pending on which way a bet has been made. Yet he has a
good deal of importance, actually—and perhaps even
more than usual in a bout on such a mammoth scale as
this one was obviously turning out to be.

Both sides, therefore, gave the matter a lot of thought,
although there wasn't much they could do about it. In
the end, the selection of the referee was up to the Illinois
State Athletic Commission.

After one of his final workouts, Tunney sat down with
Jimmy Bronson and Billy Gibson and talked about it.
Paramount in their minds was trying to plump for a
referee who was "unreachable" by hoods.

Dave Miller, Bronson felt, would be a good one. "He's
a Shriner, same as me," Jimmy said, "and he wouldn't
double-cross a lodge brother." Gibson was a little doubtful, and then Bronson turned to Tunney.

"There's no use in worrying about this thing," he said.
"I think any Chicago referee will be on the square. There
is too much at stake for any crookedness in front of
all those people. It would be professional suicide."

Bronson paused. "But there's one referee I hope is not
appointed to referee this fight and I'd hold out against
him if I were you."

Tunney asked the referee's name.

"Dave Barry. He's honest, but I know he doesn't like
me. I'd feel more comfortable if he were not the third
man."

John Righeimer, chairman of the State Athletic Commission, seemed as determined as anyone to have a good
man working as the third person in the ring. Before the
bout, he visited Edward Kelly to reassure him. Kelly was
the chairman of the South Park Board of Commissioners,

227

which controlled Soldier's Field and had leased it to Rickard for the bout.

"No hoodlum is going to referee the fight," Righeimer told Kelly, "and I will tell you the name of the man if you want me to."

"I don't care to know his name," Kelly said. "My only concern is that he is not a hoodlum."

The newspapers stepped into the problem, too. The Chicago *Herald-Examiner* sent a reporter to the Athletic Commission's offices with a message from its publisher: the paper would "not tolerate" the appointment of a referee of bad reputation. If such a one *were* named, the *Herald-Examiner* would do everything in its power to have Righeimer removed from office.

WITH CHICAGO'S unsavory reputation at the time, it was impossible, of course, that the rumors about "business" and "fix" and "dives" would not mushroom.

Later Dempsey was to say that he had been approached in Chicago by a person who told him that for payment of $125,000 he'd be assured of victory. No mention was made of it at this time, however, and Tunney claimed no one had approached him—nor ever had, during his entire career, he added.

Anton Cermak, Tunney's sometime golfing partner, who was later to die in Miami of an assassin's bullet aimed at Franklin D. Roosevelt, was then chairman of the Cook County Board of Commissioners. As the stories of alleged gamblers' intervention in the fight got stronger and bigger, he got out of a sickbed and went over to Tunney's camp to talk over the situation with Gene and his aides. Afterward Cermak had a very frank talk with Kelly.

Since Kelly's board had the power to rescind its permission to Rickard to stage the fight, it might be better to do so, Cermak philosophized, rather than have a scandal.

Kelly replied that of course he, too, had heard the rumors but hadn't pinned any of them down. He did know Capone had bet on Dempsey and he knew that a brother of Dave Miller, one of the possible referees, had bet $50,000 on Jack.

Simultaneously, Frank ("I Am the Law") Hague, the Mayor of Jersey City and an old acquaintance of Tunney's, got into the picture. The day before the bout, he came to Chicago and promptly telephoned Gene.

"There's a rumor going around Chicago that you are going to lose by a knockout in the seventh round," Hague said. "I know this is not true, but I want to know what kind of shape you are in. There are all kinds of rumors about an injury to your eye, to your hands, and I want you to tell me if there is anything to these rumors."

Tunney felt Hague sounded sincere. "Mayor," he replied, "I do not know anything about the rumors. If I am knocked out in the seventh round, it will be because Dempsey knocked me out. There will be no feigning on my part."

It had been many a long year—Corbett, perhaps?—since there had been a boxer who knew the meaning of the word "feigning."

Hague reported the result of his phone conversation to Kelly, adding his own opinion that someone or some group was trying to do some juggling with the fight, even though Dempsey and Tunney had no part in it. "There's an awfully persistent report," Hague said, "that the biggest scoop in betting history may be being plotted."

229

There was no doubt that if such a plot was in the wind, it *would* be the biggest ever staged. All over the world, people were betting on the fight. Jack Doyle's $10,000,000 estimate for the United States was a modest figure when betting elsewhere in the world was taken into consideration.

Kelly went twice to Righeimer's office and warned him of the importance of the fight being aboveboard and, again, of a good referee being named. "The hoodlums are planning a steal," Kelly said. "If any man of bad reputation is put in that ring as referee, I am going to expose the whole thing. I warn you, I have already written a statement for release to the press and in it have stated that this sinister plot has been called to your attention by me."

There seemed little doubt that the commissioners on all the commissions were worried over the "sinister plot." Presumably Rickard would have enjoyed having such publicity spread around about the fight—fight fans normally love to go and see a fixed bout, just to say they were there—but actually there wasn't that much in the newspapers about it.

ON WEDNESDAY, September 21, there was a conference in the offices of the Athletic Commission about rules interpretation. Tunney sent three men to represent him— Bronson, Gibson and George Whiteside. Whiteside, a dignified gray-haired lawyer who wore chamois gloves and carried a Malacca cane, was attached to the firm of Chadbourne, Stanchfield and Levy, which handled some of Gene's business.

Getz was there and so was Flynn, for Dempsey.

Although later Bronson said he had brought up the

point, most agreed that it was Flynn who said, "Now about knockdowns. I want it understood that in the event of a knockdown, the man scoring it should go to the farthest neutral corner. If he refuses, the count will not begin until he has done so. Right? In other words, he's penalized by the count being held up until he goes there, the penalty being for disobeying the rule."

Flynn was right, of course, and all present agreed. The rest of the conference was more or less routine, although at one point Flynn turned to Whiteside and exclaimed, "For God's sake, let's be frank. I'm here to steal as much for my man as I can. Why don't you admit the same?"

Whiteside, who for years had been with William Travers Jerome in the New York District Attorney's office, was astonished. "What!" he said. "That's just *why* I'm here—to prevent your stealing anything!"

The foul question was brought up briefly, and Righeimer ruled that the referee could not immediately disqualify a fighter who fouled. If physicians checked the allegedly fouled boxer and found no sign of such a thing, he said, the bout would go on.

It was decided further that the boxers' hands would be taped in the dressing rooms, each man being fitted out in the presence of a Commission inspector and two representatives of the rival boxer. The taping called for ten yards of 2½-inch surgeons' gauze and six feet of 1½-inch tape "to be fairly distributed."

The referee and judges, it was decided, were to write out their verdict slips immediately after the fight and pass them on to Commissioners Righeimer, Prehn and Luzzo. If the Commissioners approved them, they would be given to the announcer.

The seconds were decided upon. In Tunney's corner

would be Bronson, Gibson, Fink and Lou Brix. In
Dempsey's, Flynn, Billy Duffy, Jerry the Greek and Joe
Benjamin.

ON THURSDAY, September 22, the two men broke camp
and went into town to await the fight.

Tunney spent the early part of the day reading and
talking with newsmen. He said he planned to give a ticket
to the bout to each disabled Marine veteran in Chicago,
and when the reporters asked him to make a prediction,
he didn't hesitate.

"My first defense of the title finds me quite confident I
will be victorious," he said.

Dempsey ran three miles on the road in the morning,
then spent a couple of hours with his cousins, the Copleys
of West Virginia, and with Mayor C. Clarence Heslen of
Salt Lake City. "I'll knock that big bookworm out inside
of eight rounds," he told the reporters. "If Tunney thinks
I plan to do it with my left hook, he'll be surprised. This
time I'm going to drop him with my right."

To which Leo Flynn added, as an amen, "It'll go three
rounds if Tunney fights like a champion should. A few
more, if he runs away."

Dr. Robert R. Shea, Tunney's personal physician, gave
Gene a last-minute check and said he was in such good
shape that he, Shea, was going out to bet $2000 on him.

When Dempsey left by car for the bungalow atop the
Morrison Hotel in town—the same accommodations
once occupied by President Coolidge—he waved to the
few remaining sparmates at the racetrack camp. "Get
even, boys," he called out. "I'm going to win."

It was a clear and cool day. All roads led to Chicago.

CHAPTER 16

"WHATEVER PLACE the year 1927 may take in history," *The New York Times* said in an editorial it called "The Thrill Hunters," "no future chronicler of our times can fail to note that people will contribute about three million dollars to see two men fight for something less than forty-five minutes.

"It will not only be an index of the prosperity of the period, but it will reveal to the historian how much the twentieth century American was willing to pay for a thrill."

Yet it was not only in America. It was, to all intents and purposes, the same the world over.

In Berlin the fight was the lead story in all the newspapers. In London it was the same, the difference being that in Germany Dempsey was favored and in England Tunney was favored. Dempsey was, however, the sentimental choice in England, perhaps because of the many friends he had made with his modesty and good manners during his visit to London. The British took the "fix" and "dive" rumors with a wry smile, remembering the way Doc Kearns so recently had built up the Walker-Milligan fight with publicity. (He had rejected all the referees suggested and demanded that the Prince of Wales be the third man in the ring.)

In Shanghai the clubs and hotels were jammed with people trying to get close to the radios. In Rio de Janeiro hundreds thronged into Carioca Square, pushing toward the newspaper offices to read the bulletins. In San Juan thousands of persons made ready for the wireless reports in plazas, clubs and theaters. (They were to be amazed at the clarity of reception; Puerto Ricans said they could hear the shuffle of the boxers' feet.)

Hundreds of passengers aboard the *Berengaria,* in mid-Atlantic, 1500 miles from Chicago, huddled around a "Radiola Twenty" to hear the fight, and from Schenectady, New York, the broadcast of the powerful radio station 2XAF was picked up in England. In Lima, Peru, the corridors of *El Commercio* and other papers were filled with thousands of Peruvians seeking news of the bout.

In Cape Town, South Africa, thousands of persons stayed up all night; the news of the verdict was to come through to them at 5:50 a.m. South African time. And, perhaps most remarkable, 6000 men and women crowded in front of *El Telégrafo* in Guayaquil, Ecuador, waiting for a simple Associated Press flash on the verdict.

In the United States the radio broadcast was heard in some unlikely places. The thirteenth annual show of the

American Dahlia Society was being held at the 104th Field Artillery Armory in New York City, but after an auction of flowers the rest of the show was canceled for the night so the visitors could hear the fight.

At the New Jersey State Prison in Trenton, all but four of the 500 inmates were permitted to listen. The four were in death row. At Sing Sing, in New York, acting warden John Sheehy was more lenient. He let all the male convicts hear the broadcast, including the fifteen in the death house; and through a door left open between the men's and women's cells, Mrs. Ruth Snyder, the nation's most notorious prisoner, sat on her bunk and listened. She was scheduled to be executed for the murder, with Judd Gray, of her husband in the year's most sensational crime.

There were great crowds along Broadway in New York and some of them crowded into sightseeing busses equipped with radios as barkers cried, "Hear the fight for fifty cents." The legitimate theaters were half empty as New York, like the rest of America, stayed home. The show houses reported $1000 to $1500 below normal gross receipts each.

The whole world seemed to have gone slightly silly. It may have been at its silliest at the 71st Regiment Armory in New York City. There two boxers named Bernie Hufnagle and Andy Williams, one in black tights to represent Dempsey and the other in white to portray Tunney, entertained a sizable crowd by re-enacting the bout as the round-by-round reports came over the telegraph wires.

As EVENING CAME, it was almost impossible to walk along the sidewalks in the Loop, so great were the crowds. Michigan Boulevard had the aspect of a log jam. Thousands upon thousands of Chicagoans without tickets were drawn, as if magnetized, toward Grant Park and Soldier's Field, but there was little satisfaction waiting them there. The park had been cleared of people and cars during the day, and a police line had been set up four blocks from the ring. Anyone crossing the bridges to Grant Park, the orders read, had to have a fight ticket in his possession.

From all ends of the nation the fight buffs swept in.

Some, like Herbert Bayard Swope, the editor of *The World,* came in their own private railroad cars. Swope had journeyed to Philadelphia for the first Dempsey-Tunney bout in Harry F. Sinclair's private car, but this time he hired his own, at a cost of a bit more than $3000. He had sixteen front-row seats for his party, which included Joshua Cosden, J. Leonard Replogle, Harold Talbott, Charles Schwartz and Harry Payne Whitney. They had put together a pool on the fight's outcome, as the train neared Chicago. When it was learned that it totaled only $30,000, Swope (who was a Tunney man and picked him in the pool) added his personal check for $20,000 to make it an even $50,000.

A few came by plane—Thomas Cook and Sons had chartered some aircraft—but the majority poured in by auto and train. The Twentieth Century Limited was three times its normal length. Nine American governors arrived, one of them, Fred W. Green of Michigan, by plane. Others who flew to Chicago included William B. Leeds, Jr., the New York socialite, and his wife, the Princess Xenia of Greece; and Phil Brown, owner of the St. Louis Browns baseball team.

They came from the rest of the world. A man named John H. Grant made his way to Soldier's Field after a trip from Shanghai, and another, H. M. Reed, traveled from Mangalore, India. Still one more was a Cape Town merchant.

Not everyone was there, of course. In Bloomingdale, New Jersey, the two daughters of Mr. and Mrs. John Cook couldn't get away—but they did manage to postpone their double wedding until Saturday so they could listen to the bout. One of the bridegrooms, the story went, had money on the contest. Police Chief John Wise of Lima, Ohio, and George C. Reiter of Canton started by auto for Chicago, but were killed en route when their car turned over on the highway.

But the names, names, Names.

Doug Fairbanks, for example, was an early arrival; he leaped over three cops and a railing to get into his seat. Jack Johnson was present, flashing his gold smile. Phil Wrigley, the baseball magnate and chewing-gum heir, was told sharply by an usher to make way for a retail-furniture dealer from Toledo, and he said meekly, "Yes, sir, right away." The Marquis of Clydesdale was on hand and he, too, got the snappish "Move along, me lad" treatment from the ushers.

Doc Kearns was present to see Dempsey fight for the third time in his later career without Doc in his corner. Adolph Zukor, Mrs. Vincent Astor, Mr. and Mrs. Marshall Field, Irvin S. Cobb, Assistant Secretary of War Hanford MacNider, Amon Carter (with a party of twenty-nine friends), Jesse Livermore, Alfred P. Sloan, Jackie Coogan, Jim Jeffries, Jim Corbett, Benny Leonard, Battling Nelson, Tom Sharkey, Paolino, Johnny

Dundee, Bernard Baruch, Clarence Mackay were all there. . . . The names went on and on. One-eyed Connolly, the gate crasher, was on hand again, crouching at first by the edge of the ring but later shunted back to the $30 seats to do his crouching.

Twelve hundred press tickets finally had been given out for the event, and the veteran sportswriters and columnists, the ones who had lived and talked and played cards for weeks with the boxers, began drifting in. Nearly all of them were in their seats by the time the first preliminary went on, between Big Boy Peterson and Johnny Grosso, about eight o'clock.

The early part of the day had been fair. Now it had become gray and overcast, and before the Peterson-Grosso fight was over, a light rain had started falling. It was a Chicago autumn evening, and there were overcoats, furs, stadium blankets and windbreakers everywhere.

Graham McNamee, the excitable radio announcer, huddled in his little space by ringside and looked around at the mass of humanity. When he started his broadcast he would say, almost in wonder, "All is darkness in the muttering mass of crowd beyond the light. It's like the Roman Colosseum."

But one of the reporters (who got no byline on his story) waxed more eloquent:

"The veil of darkness over it all; the rippling sea of humanity stretching out as far as the eye could see; the Doric columns of Soldier's Field glowing a soft white along the upper battlements of the arena; and finally the ring itself where two men would fight it out with their fists in a pool of white light—these were the high spots of an unforgettable spectacle."

Paul Gallico, the columnist of the New York *News,* was an early bird in his seat. He opened his portable typewriter and, leaning back, thought about the magic of Dempsey. "Rickard played the cards," Gallico said, "but the ace of spades was, as it always is, the highest card in the deck. Dempsey was it." He thought about the five $1,000,000 gates in boxing history—and how Jack had been involved in all of them, twice with Tunney, and once each with Carpentier, Firpo and Sharkey. A total of $8,600,000 had been grossed in those five bouts.

For this one the official count would be 104,943 spectators and receipts of $2,658,660. Tunney would receive just a bit over $990,000 as his end (he was to write his personal check for the difference and give it to Rickard so he would have the fun of holding a check for a million dollars in his hand). Dempsey's end, $425,000, would be the greatest ever paid to a non-champion in a fight.

Looking around, Gallico could tell that the crowd was with Dempsey. In the first fight Jack had been the villain, but the tables had turned and "Tunney suddenly found himself pictured a priggish, snobbish, bookish fellow, too proud to associate with common prizefighters."

Gallico himself had a leaning toward Dempsey, for his warmth and good nature, which the sportswriter had experienced at first hand. When Jack was training for Firpo at Saratoga, Gallico had put on the gloves and boxed with him, to write about it. The columnist "escaped through the ropes, shaking, bleeding a little from the mouth, with resin dust on my pants and a vicious throbbing in my head." Dempsey, almost totally unable to pull a punch against anyone, had knocked Gallico kicking—but then had clinched, held up the writer and whispered, "Wrestle around a bit, son, until your head clears."

Gallico waited with a little sadness for Dempsey to show in the ring. He was thinking about the old Dempsey training camps, such as "Crying Tom" Luther's place at Saratoga, where there were "sparring partners with bent noses and twisted ears, Negroes and white fighters, boxing writers, handsome state troopers in their gray and purple uniforms; doubtful blondes who wandered in and out of the layout of wooden hotel and lake-front bungalows, and blondes about whom there was no doubt at all; a lady prizefighter; old semi-bald Uncle Tom, always crying and complaining over the Gargantuan pranks of the sports writers; and Jack Kearns, smart, breezy, wise-cracking, scented, who virtually tore the hotel apart.

"It was gay, low, vulgar, Rabelaisian and rather marvelous."

It hadn't been that way this summer. The camp at Lincoln Fields, even with Joe Benjamin around us the court jester, had been "the quietest and dullest of all." "He [Dempsey] was then no longer the ignorant, hungry, inarticulate, half-savage fighter," Gallico wrote. "He had grown into a man."

When Tunney and Dempsey went to the dressing rooms to make ready, there were no more statements, no more displays of confidence, no more of anything except to dress, take a deep breath and prepare to follow the cordon of policemen up to the ring. Dempsey had gone back to the Morrison after the afternoon weigh-in at the Illinois Athletic Club, and his only visitor had been Estelle. Together they had given out a statement that seemed a little bizarre for the rough-and-ready Jack, and most of the writers assumed Estelle had written it: "We face the issue in calm confidence. May we, from the vantage of our dear fireside, look back on one of life's great satisfactions, the good job well done." It almost sounded like a Tunneyism.

Estelle, as usual, was not at Soldier's Field. With her nurse she was locked in the Edgewater Beach suite, where, early in the fight, she was to order the radio shut off and then lock herself in the bathroom until the eighth round, when the nurse would coax her out.

In Tunney's dressing room Gus Wilson and another Dempsey aide watched Gene's hands being bandaged. Tunney had wanted the bandaging done in the ring but had been overruled.

Jimmy Bronson, although hated by the Dempsey camp, went to Jack's dressing room with Police Captain Mike Grady and Lou Brix. A police sergeant, Tappscott, tried to block Bronson from entering. Grady pushed forward and jabbed a finger into the sergeant's chest. "Listen, flatfoot," he barked, "I'm giving you your choice. Either shut your face or I'll—" He moved a hand toward his hip.

The sergeant looked at him stonily.

"Yeah," Grady said, pointing to a ventilation window high up on the wall, "yeah, shut up—or I'll make you climb out through that window. See?"

Bronson stayed.

There was splendor in and around the ring. The ring posts themselves were gilded, and in place of the usual battered water buckets in the corners, there were gold-painted containers swinging on hinges from the posts. There were evening clothes, wrinkling a little under the persistent rain, everywhere. Tex Rickard, standing in an aisle with Hype Igoe, the sportswriter and publicity man, looked happier than anyone had ever seen him.

"Kid," he said slowly to Igoe, "if the earth came up and the sky came down and wiped out my first ten rows, it would be the end of everything. Because I've got in those ten rows all the world's wealth, all the world's big men, all the world's brains and production talent. Just in them ten rows, kid. And you and me never seed nothing like it."

The ushers wore armbands that read *Tunney-Dempsey Boxing Exhibition*. Mr. Rickard had created his masterpiece and he had given it an appropriate, if rather incongruous, background.

Around ten o'clock the boxers came to the ring.

DEMPSEY WAS the first to arrive. Wearing black trunks and his old black-and-white-checked bathrobe, he climbed through the ropes surrounded by a small army of seconds and hangers-on—the police sergeant Tapscott, Flynn, Jerry the Greek, Gus Wilson, Billy Duffy and others. He jogged around near his corner, waved to friends and looked relaxed. He had a three-day stubble on his face, and a month of work under a hot sun had baked him a deep tan. If you looked quickly, without seeing the added bulk on his great physique, you could almost imagine the wildcat of Toledo, circa 1919.

Tunney, although he said later it was unintentional, kept Dempsey waiting for a few minutes. When he finally climbed up the ringside steps, he was clad in his blue-

and-scarlet bathrobe with the Marine Corps emblem on it, and wore white trunks. He had an Irishman's whiteness to his body that contrasted sharply with the Dempsey tan.

Dempsey went over and smiled at the other. "How are you, Gene?" he said.

"Quite well, Jack—and you?" Tunney replied.

They grinned politely. They had observed the amenities.

The gloves were brought to ringside in boxes tied with blue ribbon. They were put onto the two men's hands as the inevitable parade of other boxers being introduced to the crowd began to cross the ring, to the machine-gun counterpoint of Joe Humphreys' announcing. Then they were cleared away, and Humphreys, for the first time seeming a little awed by what he found himself mixed up in, roared out, "This is a fight for the world's heavyweight championship!"

THAT WAS when the roaring began. For weeks, months, a year, the thousands who were sitting in the stadium on the edge of Lake Michigan in the rain had been waiting for this moment, and here it was. They started yelling, almost howling, from ringside to the cheapest seats nearly a quarter of a mile away—and, for an hour, never stopped. Sometimes the roar softened a little, but always it was there, swelling or abating. George M. Cohan was yelling and so were Ralph Pulitzer, John Ringling, Norma Talmadge, Buster Keaton, Irving Berlin and Fatty Arbuckle.

Corporation presidents and garbage men, everday movie-goers sitting next to—and scarcely noticing—their film idols; all of them were howling, unmindful of the drizzle. Hunched over his typewriter, Grantland Rice marveled. "Never again," he wrote, "will I witness the mass of seething humanity that jammed Soldier's Field. Typewriters snarled, their keys endeavoring to outdo the next machine with bombastic descriptives and double superlatives."

Humphreys announced the officials—and Tunney swallowed hard. The judges were a couple of Chicago businessmen, George Lytton and Sheldon Clark . . . and the referee was gray-haired Dave Barry, the man Jimmy Bronson had said "is honest but doesn't like me."

At 10:07 p.m. Barry called the men to the center of the ring. Flynn and Jerry the Greek accompanied Dempsey; Gibson and Bronson were with Tunney. Barry looked all business. "Both you boys have received a book of rules of this boxing commission," he said. "They are the rules under which you are going to fight. They have been discussed by your representatives, I understand, for several days at the commission."

Flynn and Gibson nodded.

"The rabbit and kidney blows are barred, of course," Barry said. "Now I want to get this one point clear. In the event of a knockdown, the man scoring the knockdown will go to the farthest neutral corner. Is that clear, Jack? Is that clear, Champ?"

Both men nodded yes. *Champ,* Tunney thought. It was the first time he could remember having been called that. Always "Champ" had been only one man, Dempsey.

"Now," Barry went on, "in the event of a knockdown, unless the boy scoring it goes to the farthest neutral corner, I will not begin the count." Again he asked if that was clear and again they nodded. "When I tell you to break," he added, "I want you to break clean and step back without hitting." Then he took a long pause and looked closely at the two.

"Shake hands now and come out fighting," Barry said.

THEY CAME OUT fighting. Not pushing, mauling, shoving, swinging, not club-fighting. They moved professionally, jabbing, hooking, always their eyes on each other. The good ones don't look too closely at the other's arms, fists or feet. They watch the eyes. Any fighter, even the most skillful, begins a punch, fast or slow, wide or in close, with the expression in his eyes.

It was a different Dempsey from Toledo. Jack boxed and wove and kept circling. People had forgotten, or perhaps never had realized, that he was one of the best natural boxers. His footwork was impeccable, his timing beautiful and his balance beyond criticism.

If he had a drawback, beyond age and the inroads of easy living, Tunney had pegged it: "Dempsey's only drawback, really, was lack of a cold brain. He was not a reasoning, thinking fighter."

Dempsey's weaving and circling seemed to be working. Midway through the first round Tunney drove him to the ropes with a left-and-right combination to the jaw, but for a good part of the round Tunney was missing him with right-hands. The champion seemed overanxious, yet he kept himself rigidly under control and, even with the rights he was missing, jolted Dempsey with left-hands frequently.

In the second, Jack staggered Tunney mildly with a good left hook to the head. In the third, Dempsey began

245

to step up the pace. He was definitely the aggressor, and one of the newsmen jotted down a note on his scratch paper: "Tunney in full flight." It wasn't quite like that; the champion was counterfighting and scoring, but it *was* true that Dempsey was pressing. A couple of his punches strayed a little low, and Barry warned him.

Tunney kept firing the rights, hoping to straighten them out, hoping to bring Dempsey up from his crouch —and near the end of the fourth round he landed one on Jack's temple. Dempsey went back into a neutral corner, his right eye cut, and looked unsteady as the bell rang.

Tunney, comparatively fresh in his corner, looked over at the other and thought he had a good chance of finishing Dempsey off in the fifth. "I may even knock him out," he had told the reporters back at the Cedar Crest camp.

It wasn't like that. Dempsey might have been soft by Dempsey standards, but his recuperative powers still were with him. He came out for the fifth seemingly as fresh as ever and once again he moved forward as Tunney went backward. Still weaving, still hard to hit, Jack scored with some hard shots to the body—but as the round wore on, Tunney began to sharpshoot again and he staggered Dempsey again with two separate rights to the jaw.

Dempsey was bleeding from two cuts on the face now. Tunney kept fashioning his artistic boxing exhibition, and he thought it would be only a question of time.

Both boxers were performing as if out of a textbook. They were heavyweights, but they might have been middleweights. Both seemed enormously careful. For one thing, Tunney knew that never as long as he was in the

246

ring with Dempsey would he grow overconfident. One mistake with a man of that potential, he felt, and you could be through.

Tunney kept trying to get at Jack's jaw, tucked down behind his shoulder as it so often was. Dempsey was attempting to fire long, straight right-hands over Tunney's left leads. Neither strategy worked too well. Gene's rights landed high and Dempsey's countering rights were missing or just sideswiping Tunney's chin.

In close, Gene kept tying Dempsey up. It wasn't that he didn't like to fight inside. He was just trying to keep clear of Dempsey's rabbit punches. Barry kept warning Jack about them, but he seemed to pay no mind. The rabbit punch, aimed at the back of the neck, hits the meetingplace of the base of the skull and the cervical vertebra—the medulla oblongata, doctors call it. Actually it is the nerve center, the center of life, and heavy blows there can cause numbness, deadening headaches and a serious twisting of this "brain stem."

Between the fifth and sixth rounds Sergeant Bill Smith, the Chicago cop hovering around Tunney's corner, climbed to the outer platform of the neutral corner where Barry was making notes on the fifth round. "You blankety-blank!" Smith yelled. "If you don't stop those rabbit punches, you'll be carried out of here dead!"

Tunney's handlers wanted to protest officially, but Gene shook his head. "Don't bother," he insisted. "I'm O.K."

They came out for the sixth and Tunney marveled at the way Dempsey, bleeding and obviously tiring, kept coming forward, still boxing, still throwing punches. He remembered watching Dempsey knock out Sharkey and how he had felt that Jack had out-gamed the Boston sailor. Jack's left ear was cut now and his left eye was swelling, but he didn't slacken. He drummed punch after punch to Tunney's body, then shifted up to score with lefts and rights to the jaw. Tunney seemed well ahead on points, but he didn't have the fight wrapped up by any means. He still was wild with his rights, wild and short.

THEY CAME OUT for the seventh and both men jabbed, feinted, clinched, broke and circled again for about fifty seconds.

Tunney, still in his classic pose, led with a straight left and this time Dempsey crossed over it with a long right and landed, high. Tunney went back a step or two, Jack following, He threw a long swinging left hook and it caught Tunney on the right side of the chin. It was Dempsey's best shot of the night and Tunney felt it. He shook his head and felt angry with himself for being hit with a sucker punch, but there was no time for meditation. Dempsey came in with another right, which Gene rode with partially, back to the ropes. Somewhat relaxed, he came off the ropes, raising his guard—and Dempsey slipped inside it with another left hook. It was a vicious shot and it caught Tunney coming in.

The four punches, delivered almost triphammer-like, told on Tunney and he sagged back against the ropes. He tried to clutch one for support and Dempsey was after him. For just a moment, for just a moment of the dark wet night in Chicago, he was the Dempsey of Toledo. He swung a right, a left, a right, and Tunney tumbled down. Or, rather, collapsed, like a building falling to the wrecker's ball.

248

"I thought he was finished," Dempsey was to say later. "I thought I had become the first guy ever to win back the heavyweight title after blowing it. I hit him with all the punches I had been trying to hit him with in the ring and in my sleep for the past year."

The roar of the crowd was beyond imagining now; 105,000 persons were on their feet, jumping, stamping, waving, yelling. Holding tightly to his microphone, McNamee seemed to be turning apoplectic. "Some of the blows that Dempsey hits make this ring tremble!" he shouted. "TUNNEY IS DOWN! DOWN FROM A BARRAGE! . . . THEY ARE COUNTING! . . ."

Knocked out? Tunney? To be sure, he was—but you can be knocked out for two seconds or four or forty.

Almost as soon as he hit the floor, Tunney reached up with his left hand and caught hold of the lower rope to pull himself into a sitting position. It was instinct. You had only to look at his blue eyes to know he was scrambled and at sea. Or, as he said later himself, "I have no recollection of the last three punches."

And Dempsey?

He stepped back, his mind churning, and went to the nearest corner and stood there with his arms across the top rope. He looked down at Paul Beeler, the knockdown timekeeper, who had begun his count—and then he saw Barry rushing over to him.

"Go to a neutral corner, Jack!" the referee yelled, but Dempsey stared at him, scowling.

"I stay here," he said. Wasn't that enough concession? In so many of his other bouts, before the rules said otherwise, he had stood over his opponents, ready to hit them as soon as their knees were off the floor. Now at least he had backed off a little. But Barry grabbed him and shoved him toward the neutral corner across the ring, and, finally, Jack shuffled over there.

When Barry got back to Tunney and crouched over him, Beeler—as he said later—was calling out "Five." Barry looked at him quickly and shouted, "One!" and Beeler, reacting, changed his next call to "Two."

The bedlam was unbelievable—and in the front row, one Chicago newspaperman waved and shouted at Tunney, "Get up, you quitter!" Others, dictating to their telegraph men, remembered suddenly the stories of the "fix": Dempsey to win in the seventh round.

Nat Fleischer, the little bald editor of *The Ring* magazine and one of the few genuine boxing experts on hand, leaned forward and looked closely at Tunney. Barry had reached four—that would be eight or nine by Beeler's original count—and Tunney, Fleischer felt, was "still weak and glassy-eyed." But as the count went on, second by second, Tunney's great physical condition swept him back to the land of the living.

"It seemed plausible," Fleischer wrote later, "that he could get up at ten. By then, he was not groggy."

In Tunney's corner "Bow-tie Jimmy" Bronson and Gibson, their eyes nervous and wild, waved to him to stay down and take a nine count. Through his clearing eyes Gene saw them and nodded. He was a professional, and the professionals take as much time on the floor as they're allowed.

His mind worked quickly. He had worked out, before the bout, two plans for just such a situation. One was to clinch and hold, when he got up. "But now," he said later, "I had to dismiss this first alternative because of the danger of Dempsey's rabbit blow, which I knew he would use if I attempted to clinch, and which would probably cause a complete collapse."

The other plan was to gamble. A fighter who has knocked down another, and smells triumph, often wades in wildly—leaving himself open. A good shot can turn the tide.

But Tunney by now had boxed seventeen rounds with Dempsey—and never once had landed a hard punch on his jaw, which is where the gambling punch would have to go. Dempsey, he now knew so well, fought almost instinctively with his head tucked against his chest.

Two plans—both had to go out the window.

Barry started to count ten—and Tunney got up . . . and followed plan three: retreat. He feinted and moved, circled and back-pedaled. Gene Fowler, sitting at ringside, nodded approvingly. "It is dangerous," he dictated to his telegrapher, "to miss Dempsey with any sort of blow. Dempsey, always pictured as an aggressive, tearing, weaving, inside battler, is himself a great counterfighter."

Even as the two men kept at it, Tunney retreating and Dempsey following, the arguments were beginning to rage. Stopwatches had been clicked as soon as Tunney had hit the canvas—and now their owners were yelling that he had been down from twelve to seventeen seconds. Later, Fleischer was to quote Beeler: "Tunney was on the floor exactly thirteen seconds, which, with the one-second final count as he arose, made the full count fourteen."

Or, as Dempsey put it, "Tunney took the count, whatever it was. And that's what any smart fighter would have done. In boxing, take what they give you."

Dempsey, crouching, his left hand almost on the floor, pushed after Tunney. He threw the left savagely—and Gene picked it off and circled to Jack's right. Tunney went completely around the ring in retreat, ducking eight or nine of Dempsey's desperate swings. He knew by now this would work. But his mind still was turning over. He decided it was time to try to fight back.

He slowed a little and Dempsey neared. Then Tunney hit him with a straight right-hand to the temple. They closed and counterpunched five or six times. Parting, they resumed the chase—and then Tunney came in with another straight right and hit him on the chin.

Then in a gesture that said it all to those in the crowd looking carefully, Dempsey gave away the key to the fight, the night, the times, the spectacle.

His legs, it seemed, had failed him. He couldn't catch Tunney. "Over his swarthy, blue-jowled fighter's face," Paul Gallico wrote, "there spread a look, the memory of which will never leave me as long as I live. First it was the expression of self-realization of one who knows that his race is run, that he is old and that he is finished. . . . With his gloves, Dempsey made little coaxing, pawing motions to Tunney to come in and fight. That was it. Don't run. Come in and fight. This is a fight."

For that, Gallico added, was "what Dempsey would have done." In his fights against Firpo and Sharkey, for instance, when he was in trouble, "his instincts were yet to move forward, close with the enemy and fight."

Tunney was to call it later "a grandstand gesture. . . . Here was I, just up from a count," he said, "and, while avoiding his attempts to put me down again for keeps, being beckoned by my opponent to come in so that he could land the finishing punch or punches!"

Dempsey was to be more philosophical, even humorous about it. "It seems pretty silly when I look back on it," he would say, "though a lot of guys wrote some nice things about that. Why should he do what I wanted him to do?"

To Tunney it was not only a grandstand gesture, but also an acknowledgment of discouragement. He moved cautiously toward Dempsey, feinted the other into an opening, and then drove his straight right under Jack's heart. Dempsey didn't go down, but, bending forward, with his arms still close to his body, he kept weaving slowly, instinctively, until the bell rang.

"That was the hardest blow I have ever received," Dempsey later told Ray Long and Roy Howard, the publishers. "It was not a question in my mind of being knocked out. I thought I was going to die. I could not get my breath. A second rubbed away the congestion around my heart when I came back to my corner. But for that, I would not have been able to come out for the eighth round."

IN HIS CORNER between the seventh and eighth, Dempsey was worked on feverishly by his handlers and they finally got him into some kind of shape to get up and move out again under the hot lights. Tunney refused the smelling salts shoved under his nose and asked only that he be splashed with cold water.

The final three rounds were, to understate it, anticlimactic.

Also they were terribly one-sided. It was as if Dempsey

253

knew he had had the one chance and it hadn't worked. Firing his straight rights and lefts, Tunney was deadly in his sharpshooting. He rocked Jack time and again. As he admitted later, he frankly tried as hard as he could for the knockout, "but Jack was too game." Cut and black-and-blued, Dempsey kept coming.

In the eighth, Gene landed a savage hook to Dempsey's jaw and Jack went down. Tunney started for a neutral corner immediately—and, ironically, Barry this time picked up the knockdown timekeeper's count, even before Tunney got there. But it was for only a couple of seconds. Then Dempsey got laboriously to his feet and moved again at Tunney.

The ninth was all Tunney.

In the tenth, weak as he was, Dempsey still pressed the attack as he had done throughout the fight. Near the end of the road, he hooked a heavy left to Tunney's head and then, falling into a clinch, almost wrestled the other to the floor. Just before the bell Tunney snapped across a left and a right and Dempsey almost went down. But he held on and the bell rang—and they kept fighting. Only after their handlers poured into the ring from each corner did the two men separate . . . and the $2,500,000 hour in Chicago was over. Tunney had won.

SOME WHO WENT in for that sort of thing estimated that Tunney had earned $7700 while on the canvas, although it wasn't noted whether this was based on twelve or seventeen seconds down.

Throughout the United States ten deaths were attributed directly to the Dempsey-Tunney bout and five of these occurred during the seventh-round knockdown.

254

Dave Barry said it was his "impression of Tunney, after he had been knocked down, that he regained his senses in three or four seconds."

Hype Igoe declared that in his fistic-expert opinion, Tunney's ringmanship after the knockdown was "the greatest in the history of the ring."

George Bernard Shaw, who had the fight movies screened privately for him a day or two after the fight, peered closely at Tunney on the floor and shouted excitedly, "You see—his eyes have cleared!"

Tunney said later that a boxer knocked down "is the loneliest man in the world. . . . For ten years," he said, "I had visualized, time and again, what I would do in such a crisis."

"Maybe Gene could have gotten up," Dempsey was to say philosophically. "Maybe not. Everything happens for the best." And, long years later in his midtown Manhattan restaurant, he told Fred Corcoran, the golfers' representative, "You know—I never did get a good shot at him. I dazed him and he went down slowly. You know, I probably hit him too many times. You can knock a fellow out sometimes and then bring him around with another punch. I've seen it happen more than once. . . ."

The arguments were only beginning and they would stretch across the next forty years. But the long count was over.

FORTY YEARS
AFTER

IN DECEMBER OF 1967 and the early months of 1968, I had some talks with both Dempsey and Tunney, each of whom had outlasted most of the others who had been in Chicago in 1927.

For men seventy and over, they were remarkably fit. Tunney was a good deal more bulky than he had been and Dempsey had a lot of weight around his once-sloping shoulders, but each was clear-eyed and sharp of recollection.

I saw Tunney each time in his office in New York's Pan American Building, in which a huge oil of Polly Lauder, the heiress he married, covers one wall. With no false modesty, he remembered that he had felt very confident of beating Jack in their second fight.

"And I must say," he said, "I felt better about winning

in Chicago than I did in Philadelphia, just for the simple fact that I came off the floor to do it." He leaned back and looked at Manhattan, smoky and gray in the winter afternoon.

"The whole thing depended on whether my legs would carry me away when I got up after the knockdown," he added, "and they did. Soon after, I felt a hundred percent. But I must say, Jack had too much heart for me to put him away in the next three rounds, try as I might."

Dempsey, who can be found nearly every evening in the restaurant that he and sportsman Jack Amiel operate under Dempsey's name on Broadway, was shyer but still direct. He spoke quickly and to the point, and I got the impression he no longer really wanted to talk much about the events of forty years ago.

"One thing," he said, "is that Tunney was a much better fighter than a lot of people gave him credit for. He was really good. And as for the Chicago fight itself—it was the best thing that could have happened to either of us. It kept us both alive for all these years."

RIGHT AFTER the bout neither man was beautiful to see. Tunney, calm as always, had swollen lips and a bloody smear on his left cheek. His hands, which bothered him all during his career, were, he said, "frightfully sore." Jerry the Greek had to work a half-hour to fix up Dempsey, who had cuts over both eyes, a bump under the right one, a gash near the mouth and a cut on his left ear.

In the weeks, months and years following the big bout, their paths went in sharply different directions.

Tunney fought once more, in July of 1928. He knocked out Tom Heeney in the eleventh round at the

257

Polo Grounds in one of the least successful promotions in boxing history; the Madison Square Garden Corporation, which promoted the fight, reportedly lost $200,000 on it. Gene then retired undefeated, the only heavyweight champion to do so up to that time. (Rocky Marciano did it much later.) It could be that boxing started losing its popularity with that last fight of Tunney's. Today it is unheard of for 120,000 persons to attend a prizefight.

Gene married Miss Lauder in Rome in October of 1928 and, in all, they spent sixteen months in Europe. He met and got to know Hemingway—"When Hemingway is good, as in *Farewell to Arms,* nobody can touch him"—and F. Scott Fitzgerald—"He had taken to the bottle then, and he didn't drink well"—and when he returned, he became part of the business and social world he had for so long admired.

He became a director of a dozen corporations, as well as chairman of the board of the McCandless Corporation, manufacturer of rubber products, and has a 150-acre farm, "Star Meadow," in Stamford, Connecticut, where he raises white-faced Herefords.

Tunney's preoccupation with Shakespeare wasn't a publicity gimmick. He lectured on *Troilus and Cressida* at Yale—Will Rogers said, "Let's have prizefighters with harder wallops and less Shakespeare"—and he became an intimate of persons such as Shaw, Thornton Wilder and William Lyon Phelps.

In 1957 he told a veteran newsman, Jim Kilgallen, that if he were young again, he wouldn't choose to be a fighter. "Education," he said, "is the most valuable capital an ambitious youth can have nowadays."

He and his wife had four children. One of the three

boys, John V. Tunney, became a Democratic Congress-man from California, another is a banker and the third is a realtor. His daughter married a San Francisco advertising executive.

In spite of his apparent distaste for the milieu, Tunney remained a familiar figure in the fight environment after his retirement. He went to most of the big bouts, and the public's attitude, seemed to soften toward him over the years.

He has always ranked Dempsey as the greatest heavyweight fighter of all time, just in front of Bob Fitzsimmons and James J. Corbett, and he said he believed that Dempsey in his prime would have handled Joe Louis without too much difficulty.

Although a major in the Marine Corps Reserve, Tunney, at the special request of President Roosevelt, became a Navy commander during World War II and was responsible for the development of 12,500 physical-training instructors during the war.

FOR ALL PRACTICAL purposes, Dempsey retired after the Chicago fight. But he wasn't through with the ring, not really.

To begin with, he became Tex Rickard's partner. They sealed the deal with a handshake, but before they really got going together, Rickard died in a Miami hospital after an operation. Dempsey was the only one Tex would allow to visit him near the end, and the promoter died in Jack's arms.

Of his brief partnership with Tex, the fighter said, "I was as proud of that as anything in my life. He was the great man of my life."

259

Jack then became co-promoter of the Miami fight between Young Stribling and Sharkey, a bout that was highly successful despite a publicity bill of $34,000, involving the housing and feeding of 483 newsmen. Dempsey moved on to Chicago, where he promoted fights at the Coliseum, but that proved a bust.

He turned finally to refereeing and in six months earned $322,000, after which, in 1930 and 1931, he put on trunks and gloves again to stage a tour of exhibition bouts. This stretched into three separate tours, netting Dempsey more than $800,000—and Jack seemed to have at least faint hopes of returning to real action. All that ended, however, in the Chicago Stadium when a wild-swinging club fighter, King Levinsky, whose real name was Harry Krakow, defeated him easily. "He slapped me all over the ring in four rounds," Jack said bluntly.

His marriage with Estelle Taylor broke up, but left him unembittered. "She was a nice woman, really," Jack said. He married several other women, including Hannah Williams, a Broadway star noted for her singing of "Cheerful Little Earful." And, of course, he opened his restaurant, which now is a Broadway landmark.

During World War II he, too, was a commander, but in the Coast Guard. Actually he enlisted in the Army but was only in that service for ten minutes or so. A colonel accepted him, but doctors turned him down as too old (he was forty-seven). As a Coast Guard commander, however, he went to the South Pacific war zone, and on the beach at Iwo Jima was credited with capturing a Japanese soldier. His own explanation of the incident was typical. "The Coast Guard needed a picture, so they took a couple of us to a spot where some Japs were, threw a bomb—and I grabbed one of them. He must have been at least seventy." During his war career, he was awarded the Legion of Merit . . . and the word "slacker" was heard no more.

He and Tunney became fast friends, despite the ruffled feelings in the summer of 1927, and they appeared together hundreds of times at banquets, big fights and social events. Indeed, Jack did some effective campaigning for Tunney's son John when the latter was running for Congress.

The late Frank Graham, writing in the New York *Journal American,* summed up Jack's later life: " 'There goes Jack Dempsey!' they say, wherever he goes, and he's still Jack Dempsey."

BOXING, OF COURSE, went downhill, slowly but certainly. A half-dozen reasons might be advanced, but at least in the beginning it probably was the absence of a Rickard. Mike Jacobs became the premier promoter after Tex's death, and he staged some bouts that had good crowds and sizable receipts—but Jacobs never had Rickard's flair and remained, by comparison, just a minor-leaguer.

There was no Rickard, there was no Dempsey, there was no Wild Bull of the Pampas, there was no gorgeous Georges Carpentier. For a while there was Joe Louis, the incomparable, and the crowds turned out to see him, as they always will for a deadly puncher. There were others later, when Joe became fat and bald, and their names, too, became household words: Rocky Marciano, Billy Conn, Cassius Clay, Floyd Patterson, Ingemar Johansson.

But America seemed to be losing interest in the Manly Art. The crowds dwindled. The caliber of boxers, hurried along for TV purposes and unable to learn their trade the hard way over the years, slipped alarmingly. Finally the TV networks stopped carrying the weekly fight shows and boxing really was dead. In the Sixties going into the Seventies, golf and professional football seemed to be America's sports.

It was different, once.

BIBLIOGRAPHY

Caswell Adams, editor, *Great American Sports Stories* (Stamford House, 1947)

Allen Churchill, *The Great White Way* (E. P. Dutton, 1962)

———, *The Year the World Went Mad* (Thomas Y. Crowell, 1960)

Fred Corcoran, with Bud Harvey, *Unplayable Lies* (Duell, Sloan and Pearce, 1965)

Jack Dempsey, as told to Bill Slocum and Bob Considine, *Dempsey* (Simon and Schuster, 1959)

———, with Myron M. Stearns, *Round by Round* (Whittlesey House, 1940)

Donald Elder, *Ring Lardner* (Doubleday, 1956)

James R. Fair, *Give Him to the Angels* (Smith and Durrell, 1946)

Nat Fleischer, *Jack Dempsey, the Idol of Fistiana* (The Ring, Inc., 1929)

E. J. Kahn, Jr., *The World of Swope* (Simon and Schuster, 1965)

Al Laney, *Paris Herald* (Appleton-Century, 1947)

Alfred McClung Lee, *The Daily Newspaper in America* (Macmillan, 1937)

Isabel Leighton, editor, *The Aspirin Age* (Simon and Schuster, 1949)

Grantland Rice, *The Tumult and the Shouting* (A. S. Barnes, 1954)

Charles Samuels, *The Magnificent Rube* (McGraw-Hill, 1957)
Gene Tunney, *A Man Must Fight* (Houghton Mifflin, 1932)
John Wheeler, *I've Got News for You* (Dutton, 1961)

INDEX

Mel Heimer

Mel Heimer, an avid sports fan who is a good amateur tennis player and says the high point of his career came when he pitched for his high-school baseball team, has been for years one of America's most prolific authors. *The Long Count* is his thirteenth book, the others having included the novels *West Wind* and *A Family Affair* as well as *Fabulous Bawd,* a history of Saratoga, and *Pittsburgh Phil,* the story of a famous gambler of yesterday. Mr. Heimer, whose short stories have appeared in *Ladies' Home Journal, Good House-keeping, Cosmopolitan, Esquire,* and other magazines, is also a syndicated columnist for King Features. His *My New York* appears in several hundred papers and he is considered an authority on the Manhattan scene. In journalism, he has been everything from a political reporter to a night editor, and lightly says he was the poor man's H. Allen Smith when both he and Smith were rewrite men on the New York *World-Telegram.* He is widely traveled, having crossed the Atlantic forty times, was at one time an expert on jazz music and has had his poetry published in anthologies. He also is the television editor for King Features and the father of three sons.